Devotions with a Kick

MAMA T SAYS

Rise and Shine

Thelma Wells

HARVEST HOUSE PUBLISHERS

EUGENE, OREGON

Published in association with the Van Diest Literary Agency, PO Box 1482, Sisters, Oregon. www.lastchapterpublishing.com

All material presented is based on the experiences and research of the author. Some names, dates, and events have been changed to present the narrative more compactly and protect the identity of individuals involved.

Cover by Koechel Peterson & Associates, Inc., Minneapolis, Minnesota

Cover illustration © Mike Shapiro

MAMA T SAYS, "RISE AND SHINE"
Published 2009 by Harvest House Publishers
Eugene, Oregon 97402
www.harvesthousepublishers.com

Library of Congress Cataloging-in-Publication Data
Wells, Thelma.
[God will make a way]
Mama T says, "rise and shine" / Thelma Wells.
     p. cm.
     First published: God will make a way. Nashville, Tenn. : T. Nelson, © 1998. 2nd published: What's going on, Lord? Nashville, Tenn. : T. Nelson Publishers, © 1999.
     Includes bibliographical references.
     ISBN 978-0-7369-2709-3 (pbk.)
     1. God (Christianity)—Promises—Meditations. I. Wells, Thelma. What's going on, Lord? II. Title. III. Title: What's going on, Lord?
     BT180.P7W45 2009
     242'.4—dc22
                                                                        2009029467

Printed in the United States of America

09 10 11 12 13 14 15 16 17 / VP-SK / 10 9 8 7 6 5 4 3 2 1

I dedicate this book to you.

My daughter Vikki made me write this book to share with you some experiences of my heart, the scriptures I live by daily, affirmations I tell myself, and what inspires me to press on in life. She's sure these things will help you too. So maybe this book should be dedicated to her pushiness. But no, I'm going to dedicate these devotions to you.

Maybe your finances are low, your child is wayward, your relationships iffy. Or perhaps your job is questionable, your health is failing, or your heart is broken. Or could you be going along in life, everything smooth, but something is missing? Whatever your situation, please know you can "rise and shine and give God the glory" every morning because your mind is working and your heart is pumping!

So lift up your head and don't be afraid. You and I have made it this far! We've swum through treacherous waters that didn't drown us, we've walked through fires that didn't set us ablaze, and we've survived life's other catastrophes. And we're going to continue on in the name and strength of our Lord and Savior, Jesus Christ!

I care about you; I want the best for you. I want to encourage you, inspire you, and motivate you to keep your hope alive in Christ. I'm thrilled you're going to rise and shine with "Mama T"—that's me! Are you ready for some devotions that have a sweet, sometimes subtle kick to help you get started, live for God, and accomplish what you need to every day? Then let's get started. And remember: In Christ, you can BEE the best! So don't give in, God wants you to win.

Mama T

Acknowledgement

I would like to give a special thanks to my husband of more than 48 years. George is always here for me—supporting me, putting up with my sometimes crazy work hours, chauffeuring me around, and helping around the house when I need him to. His favorite saying about me, which I love, is: "I like smart women!"

George has encouraged many people and is building a legacy of fine manhood for others to emulate. He's helped many young people go into business for themselves. Always cool, calm, and collected, George's loyalty to me, his children, his grandchildren, and his great-grandchildren is never in doubt.

Inspired by good preaching, George encourages me in this regard. He tells me often that he's proud of me and my speaking ministry. We've shared many of the experiences related in this book during our marriage. I couldn't travel to speaking engagements and write like I do without his sweet consent. Other than God, he is my tower of strength. I'm honored to have him as my husband.

I love you, George!

CONTENTS

Part 2: God Will Make a Way

PART 1

What's Going On, Lord?

"For I know the plans I have for you," declares the Lord,
"plans to prosper you and not to harm you,
plans to give you hope and a future.
Then you will call upon me and come and pray to me,
and I will listen to you. You will seek me and find me when
you seek me with all your heart.
I will be found by you," declares the Lord.

Jeremiah 29:11-14

God Answers Every "What?"

One of the recurring questions asked in this section of the book is, "What's going on, Lord?" As I looked back over my life, I heard myself ask more often than I'd like to admit, "Lord, what's the problem?" "What's this about, Lord?" "What's happening here, Father?" "What's up with this, God?" "What are You trying to say, Jesus?" "What's wrong?" "What have I done to deserve this?" "What are You trying to tell me, Lord?" "What?" "What?" "What?" It seems that these questions were the greater part of my vocabulary for the first 40 years of my Christian life.

For every one of my "whats," God had an answer. When I was asked to write my first book under an extremely tight schedule, I asked God, "What? How will I make it?" But He filled my mind and heart with the words He wanted me to share. When He instructed me to quit my secure bank job to start a speaking business, I asked, "What? How will I survive?" But He prepared my husband to accept my decision and support me without regret. When my children were ready for college but our funds were low, I asked God, "What's going on? How will we provide for them?" Well, Vikki was given four years of grants and work study through the help of a concerned school counselor. George Fitzgerald was trained for his profession by a jeweler who taught him everything he knew. And Lesa was given a full scholarship to cosmetology school by a loving church member. God answered my whats. He had plans!

The Lord declared, "I know the plans I have for you...plans to prosper you and not to harm you, plans to give you hope and a future" (Jeremiah 29:11). I've learned from my experiences to rest in His peace until He reveals the answers to the whats of life.

Perhaps you have some whats in your life. You may be faced with a life-changing decision, be concerned about a loved one, face confusion about your relationship with the Lord, or are disillusioned and disappointed with people. Perhaps you feel drained from the pressures of life, frustrated with your career, and are reluctant to forgive yourself and others. Perhaps you were worried about the outcome of your circumstances so you took the situation into your own hands and messed it up. Are you at the point of giving up? Or are you patiently waiting on the Lord for an answer or solution? Whatever your situation, this book will encourage and help you.

There are testimonies of hope in this book. When you read, you'll discover faith-building strength and see the peace of God, the intercession of His Son, Jesus, and the power of the Holy Spirit bring light out of darkness, healing out of despair, cheer out of sadness, prosperity out of financial failure, strength out of weakness, forgiveness out of disappointment, truth out of misunderstood Scripture, and deliverance out of fear and anguish.

No matter what walk of life you're from, what situation you're in, what gender you are, whether you're employed or not, have a house or not, are saved or unsaved, this book is for you. My earnest prayer is you will become so convinced of God's love for you that your faith will increase and you'll have enough even during your "Lord, what's going on?" times. The apostle Paul urged, "Do not be anxious about anything, but in everything, by prayer and petition, with thanksgiving, present your requests to God. And the peace of God, which transcends all understanding, will guard your hearts and minds in Christ Jesus" (Philippians 4:6-7). Other verses also offer encouragement:

- "The way of a fool seems right to him, but a wise man listens to advice" (Proverbs 12:15).

- "There is a way that seems right to a man, but in the end it leads to death. Even in laughter the heart may ache, and joy may end in grief. The faithless will be fully repaid for their ways, and the good man rewarded for his" (Proverbs 14:12-14).

- "My God will meet all your needs according to his glorious riches in Christ Jesus" (Philippians 4:19).

- "Humble yourselves, therefore, under God's mighty hand, that he may lift you up in due time. Cast all your anxiety on him because he cares for you" (1 Peter 5:6-7).

- "Now to him who is able to do immeasurably more than all we ask or imagine, according to his power that is at work within us, to him be glory in the church and in Christ Jesus throughout all generations, for ever and ever! Amen" (Ephesians 3:20-21).

For encouragement, read this book. For hope, read this book. Give one to a family member or friend. Your church library and bookstore need to have it available. Share it with your enemies. The worst thing that can happen to them is they will be blessed. There is power in God's Word.

With a big hug to you because I love you!

Thelma

1

God Is Faithful

I have the most beautiful granddaughter. Even her name, Alaya, is beautiful. I know every grandmother thinks her grandchild is the best, brightest, and most blessed. So, yes, I'm typical. Alaya is precious! But her birth really tested my faith. You see, I prayed for her even before her mother became pregnant.

While I was attending a Christian conference with my husband, daughter, and son-in-law, my spirit was led to pray for Lesa's unborn child. That shocked my daughter. At that time she had no idea she was pregnant. She and her husband, Patrick, wanted a baby, but they had been trying to conceive for some time without success. So there I was praying for my grandchild while tears of hope and wonder streamed down my daughter's face.

A month later, Lesa and Patrick made the big announcement. I was so happy! I knew God had ordained this precious child, and that he or she was the fulfillment of God's faithfulness to Lesa and Patrick and His revelation to me.

Lesa—five feet two inches and 98 pounds—had a very easy pregnancy. But the doctor ordered her to take two weeks of bed rest near the end of her term just to be safe. On April 29, 1996, she went into labor. I was out of town for a speaking engagement when the call came. At first everything seemed normal. Lesa commented that the baby felt as if it were turning flips inside her stomach, but everyone reasoned the baby was just dropping. Then the baby's heart weakened and stopped, but the doctor was able to start it and stabilize it. They thought everything was okay...that is, until Alaya was born.

She was blue and barely able to breathe because the umbilical cord was wrapped twice around her neck. Her heartbeat was faltering. Her blood count was low. She was rushed to critical intensive care.

Not being there made the situation doubly hard for me as I determined to rest in the Lord. I wondered, *Heavenly Father, what's happening? Did You answer our prayers only to take the child back?* Mentally exhausted, my husband and I fell to our knees in prayer. While we were praying, peace that I can't explain came over me. The Holy Spirit seemed to be assuring my spirit that Alaya would not die. Because my daughter had been in prayer and praise throughout her pregnancy, I also believed God would honor her faithfulness in that hour of crisis.

But Alaya got worse. The doctor said she had reflux—an inability to retain food in her digestive tract. Although physical evidence gave little hope of her survival, I stood strong on the assurance God's Spirit had given me.

The first six days were the hardest. The doctor said the baby needed to be tested for signs of brain damage. The tests were inconclusive, but I knew she was fine. By day seven—the day of biblical completion—Alaya was released from the hospital. And today she is healthy and beautiful!

Why do I share this story? To encourage you! When you're distressed by uncertain situations—circumstances that appear to be hopeless—hold on to the fact that *God is faithful.* When you ask Him for something and believe you have received a promise from Him regarding it, trust Him! Do not doubt. God can't lie (Hebrews 6:18). He will keep His word to you.

Prayer

Father, Your faithfulness is to all generations. One thing You can't do is break a promise. Thank You for promising to keep Your promises. Give me the courage and patience to stand on Your Word even when circumstances make Your promises appear impossible. You are a God who does what He says He will do. I praise You for Your steadfast care. Amen.

God's Word to You

No matter how many promises God has made, they are "Yes" in Christ. And so through him the "Amen" is spoken by us to the glory of God. Now it is God who makes both us and you stand firm in Christ. He anointed us, set his seal of ownership on us, and put his Spirit in our hearts as a deposit, guaranteeing what is to come (2 Corinthians 1:20-22).

Affirmation

I will stand on God's promises to me
regardless of the circumstances.

2

A Calm in the Storm

A while back I talked on the phone with one of my dear friends. She was angry, fearful, exhausted, and wondering why God wasn't speaking to her and giving her directions as He had done in the past. She wanted me to explain why. But I didn't know! As I prayed for wisdom and understanding, with the aid of the Holy Spirit I shared this with her:

> My friend, when we become disappointed, angry, frustrated, and desperate, Satan can have a field day in our minds. He can load our minds with so much junk that we can't hear God or won't pay attention to the Holy Spirit when He's trying to talk to us. It doesn't matter how much we study the Bible, how long we pray, how constantly we praise God, Satan and his demons are waiting for one tiny port of entry into our minds to deceive us.
>
> Satan's job is to confuse and frustrate us to the point of retaliation, rebellion, disobedience, and distrust in God. He is always out to disturb our peace of mind while we're waiting for the manifestation of God's promises to us.

We all have storms in our lives. Perhaps a loved one is on drugs or we're experiencing physical or mental illness, financial difficulties, rejection, unemployment, painful conflict in a relationship, separation from a loved one by death or other circumstances, religious oppression, or legal trouble. I've certainly gone through some awful storms. In 1994, I asked God to give me a scripture that could be my mainstay throughout that year. He always gives me more than enough. He gave me a passage that will sustain me every day of my life:

> Do not be anxious about anything, but in everything, by prayer and petition, with thanksgiving, present your requests to God. And the peace of God, which transcends all understanding, will guard your hearts and your minds in Christ Jesus. Finally, brothers, whatever is true, whatever is noble, whatever is right, whatever is pure, whatever is lovely, whatever is admirable—if anything is excellent or praiseworthy—think about such things. Whatever you have learned or received or heard from me, or seen in me—put it into practice. And the God of peace will be with you (Philippians 4:6-9).

During the storms of our lives, we must not allow ourselves to concentrate on the frightening wind and waves around us. Remember what happened to Peter when he did that? He started to sink! (See Matthew 14:28-31.) Instead, we must direct our thoughts to the "whatevers" in the passage from Philippians. When we fix our minds on these things, we can experience God's peace and freedom from anxiety as we pass through our storms. Our hearts are guarded from becoming cynical and pessimistic. So I shared "my" verses with my friend too.

When God gave me these scriptures, I had no idea I would need them as quickly as I did. That January, the southern and northeastern states experienced their heaviest snowfall in decades. I was scheduled to speak in Pennsylvania and Ohio on two consecutive days. Travel advisories were out all over the nation, and airport closings were commonplace.

Before leaving the airport in Dallas, I called my clients in both states to find out if the sessions were still scheduled. Both clients said, "Yes, come on." When I stopped over in the Cincinnati airport on my way to Philadelphia, I called my Pennsylvania client to find out if the conference was still a go. The client told me they thought it would be wise to cancel because the airport in Philadelphia had closed indefinitely, and they weren't sure if I could make it or not. If I did get there, they couldn't guarantee that I'd be able to get out in time to make it back to Ohio to speak the next day. *Fine. That's a relief,* I thought. I quickly called the client in Ohio. "Yes," she said. "The meeting is on. We're expecting you."

By that time, the bag I checked in Dallas to go all the way to Philadelphia became a concern. I went to the baggage assistance counter of the airline to find out where my bag was. They told me it had been sent to Philadelphia. *How can that be when no flights have left the airport since I arrived?* I wondered. *I need my bags. And I'm not going to Philadelphia. I'm staying in Ohio.*

"Help me retrieve my bag," I said, beginning to whine. "All my transparencies and clothes are in that bag. I need my bag!" Just as I started to panic, I remembered my verses, "Do not be anxious about anything…" I stepped back from the counter and, with prayer and supplication, I made my petition known to God. Suddenly I felt peace. My voice became milder; my attitude calmed; I smiled again. And as I stepped back up to the counter, the agent told me he had located my luggage. It was on the plane scheduled to go to Philadelphia. It couldn't be retrieved at the moment, but he would put in an urgent request to have it returned to the baggage counter. I should check back in about three hours. Meanwhile, the airline would put me up for the night in a hotel connected to the airport. He handed me a toiletries package and a voucher for a meal, gave me directions to the hotel, and assured me that when my bag was returned, he would see that it was delivered to me. I walked away from that baggage counter with sweet peace in my spirit, believing that everything would be all right. In about five hours, I received a telephone call from the baggage claim department telling me my luggage was there and it would be sent to me at the hotel.

While I'd been standing near the baggage counter repeating my scriptures, I took a look at some of the other people standing in line. Some were shouting, cursing, demanding, and crying about their situation—the same one I was in. And I'd almost been one of those people. Tears had begun to well up in my eyes. I'd started to panic and take out my frustration on the agent. But thanks be to God! He had given me scriptures He knew I would need within a few days after receiving them.

I called my client yet a third time from Cincinnati before heading out. My rationale was that if they were going to cancel the engagement, I could return to Dallas from Cincinnati without losing much time or energy. The client assured me we were on for the program. I rented a car at the airport and drove on icy roads to get to the city where the conference was being held.

I needed my verses again when I arrived at the hotel near the site for the program. When I stepped up to the registration counter, the clerk handed me a note: "Sorry you came. We've canceled the program." I nearly went ballistic! Fortunately, I kept my mouth closed. My eyes told the desk clerk to give me a room in a hurry and to refrain from saying anything to me that might push me over the edge.

Sitting in my room, I tried to settle down. My verses came back to my mind, and I repeated them over and over until I felt calm. Once I relaxed, I was able to see the good in the situation. I could go home the next day earlier than I'd planned, and I would get paid the same money without expending any more energy and time. I would, however, *calmly* explain to the client's meeting planner how inconsiderate it was to have me come and then cancel the program after I had confirmed with her three times. Because I prayed and recited the scripture verses, my attitude was milder and more accepting than if I had not.

What a comfort to know that I don't have to go through airport delays, unwanted health reports, IRS audits, attitude adjustments, disagreements, or anything that constitutes a personal storm without God always being in charge. That airport thing was just a tiny example of some of the other times that particular Scripture passage has helped me. I've quoted it to many people during their storms and have seen it quiet their spirits and calm their fears.

Remember my frustrated friend who didn't understand why God wasn't getting through to her? Well, before we got off the telephone, she told me how much better she felt. Her circumstances were the same, but her hope was renewed and her faith increased by God's Word and His promises.

Prayer

Okay, Lord, I'm convinced. You really are in control while my storms are raging. You have the power to say, "Peace, be still" and the storm will calm. Master of everything, when I am struggling through the storms of life, please help me keep my mind on pure and righteous things. Help me realize that the storms cease more quickly when I trust in You. Thank You that I am able to speak peace to others because of Your peace in me. Amen.

God's Word to You

You will keep in perfect peace him whose mind is steadfast, because he trusts in you (Isaiah 26:3).

Affirmation

In God is my place of calm during every storm.

3

No More Monsters

I loved my great-grandfather "Daddy" Harrell. He lost his sight when I was young, and I gladly helped him get from place to place around the neighborhood. I was a brave little girl when I was leading him across the street. But at other times, I was frightened. When I closed my eyes at night I would see skeletons and bogeymen. Horrible images of monsters and scary-looking faces plagued my mind. Sometimes I'd even see them when I had my eyes open. I imagined monsters and skeletons jumping out at me and chasing me around the house. That scary time in my life went on for months.

One day a woman came to the door of our upstairs back-alley apartment and looked through the glass panel on the front door. I went into hysterics. Her face looked like the monster that had been scaring me all those months. I remember screaming and crying as Granny tried to console me. I had been around the visitor—Mrs. Jackson—all my life because she lived across the street. She'd even given me many of the pretty clothes I wore. She helped pay for my piano lessons and school supplies. I knew she wouldn't harm me, but my mind was playing tricks on me. Mrs. Jackson looked like a monster!

I thank God for Daddy Harrell. He called to me from his favorite high-back, cane-bottom chair where he sat on the screened-in front porch. He told me to lie down on the rollaway bed in the corner. Then he told me how to get rid of my nightmares and day visions of monsters and skeletons. I was to do three simple things:

1. Close my eyes.

2. Repeat the Lord's Prayer and the Twenty-third Psalm one after the other without stopping until I got relief.

3. Believe that God would make those monsters go away.

I trusted Daddy Harrell and believed everything he told me. I was scared, but I followed his instructions. The hardest thing was closing my eyes because I knew what happened almost every time I closed them.

I don't know how many times I repeated the prayer and the scripture passage as I lay on that rollaway bed. I do know I began to feel at ease. I stopped crying. I stopped feeling frightened. When I finally opened my eyes, I looked up toward the sky and saw an awesome sight. More than 40 years later, I can still see it in my mind's eye. The clouds had formed a huge figure of the head and shoulders of Jesus. He was looking upon me with pleasure, confirming to me that He had heard and answered my prayer. From that day to this, I've been free of the fear of monsters and skeletons.

When God delivered me from my nightmares, He also delivered me from the fear of being near thunder and lightning, traveling around the world alone, staying in a dark room, going out at night by myself, taking risks, and who knows what else. That's not to say I never feel frightened. Rodents are my worst fear. I hate rats! I also don't enjoy being tailgated. But being temporarily frightened doesn't compare to the horror of monsters taking over my mind.

God promises to deliver us from fear and torment, but that deliverance must be fueled by prayer, reading Scripture, faith in God, and obedience to Him. I have suggested Daddy Harrell's method of dealing with fear to my children, friends, and acquaintances because, as simple as it may seem, it gets God's attention. He is the One who told us to humble ourselves as little children as we seek His face. The process Daddy Harrell instructed me in was a simple matter of taking my mind off the problem and concentrating on God. By recalling His Word and meditating on His character, I put my mind on Jesus, and He gave me perfect peace. Now when I walk through some valleys and dark places physically, emotionally, or spiritually, I don't fear. There are no more monsters.

Prayer

God, thank You for giving me a way to be delivered from my fear and trembling. When monsterlike situations come into my life, remind me that Your Word, prayer, and counsel can relieve my apprehensions. What a mighty God You are! Amen.

God's Word to You

Even though I walk through the valley of the shadow of death, I will fear no evil, for you are with me; your rod and your staff, they comfort me (Psalm 23:4).

Affirmation

God delivers me from the "monsters" in my life and gives me peace of mind as I focus on Him.

4

The Blessing in Receiving

I love surprises! I'm delighted every time someone gives me something unexpected. I feel blessed when nice things are done to or for me. A blessing is an act of declaring or wishing God's favor and goodness upon someone. Most often, God blesses us directly or through other people when we are obedient to His commands to bless others and give of ourselves for His glory.

I enjoy giving. I often ask the Holy Spirit to direct me to people to whom I can give money—people who may not even need it but who would be blessed by my thinking of them and my gesture of giving. God regularly leads me to people and makes clear to my spirit how much to give. Sometimes the gift isn't money but other tangible and intangible gifts: an unexpected phone call, an encouraging note, a gift for no reason at all except to say "I'm thinking of you." I can't count how many times I've thought of a person's name or seen his or her face in my mind's eye. I've learned to pray for people when they come to mind or get in touch with them. There's usually something going on in their lives that they need to share.

One year I was in the Love Field Airport in Texas talking on a pay phone while waiting to board a Southwest flight to Lubbock. Two women and a little boy were sitting near me, listening to almost every word that came out of my mouth. When I finished talking, the older woman stepped up and asked, "Are you the 'Woman of God'?"

"Yes, I am. How are you?" (I knew she was referring to my TV show called *A Woman of God*…unless I just had a particularly holy glow about me that day.)

The woman and her daughter said they were frequent viewers of my show and told me how much of a blessing the program was to them. After exchanging pleasant conversation, I left them and went to get a snack. When I returned to the waiting area, the people they were meeting had just come in from Lubbock. The younger woman called me over, took her sparkling 14-karat-gold bracelet off her arm, and fastened it on my wrist. She said that while I was walking away from them, the Lord told her to bless me with that gift.

I was shocked. I'd never even seen these people before. The daughter said, "The diamonds aren't real, but I've enjoyed that bracelet. It's time for you to enjoy it. If you're ever prompted to give it to someone else, do so. It will bless her too." I continue to wear this bracelet with the spirit of love and respect in which it was given. That woman and I talk to each other by phone occasionally, and she always has an encouraging word. God used one of my viewers to bless me unexpectedly as I was obedient to do His work. Isn't He marvelous?

The speakers and staff of the New Life Women of Faith conferences have heard my bumblebee story so often that now they're on the lookout for bumblebee memorabilia. (I'll share more about my bumblebee story later. My business and personal motto is "In Christ you can be the best!") While I sit here writing this book, I can look around my sunroom and see bumblebee gifts that have been given to me from people all over the country. Elsewhere I have bumblebee soap, bath oil, dish towels, pot holders, light switch covers, flags, yard decorations—all given to me because people care and have been blessed by my ministry.

One of the most pleasant bumblebee gift surprises came my way in Pittsburgh, one Friday evening. Barbara Johnson, a bestselling author and speaker with whom I shared the platform at the "Women of Faith Joyful Journey" conferences, had found some darling bumblebee house slippers in a shop. Mary Graham, the emcee for the conference, followed Barbara's directions and surprised me with the gift of these precious bumblebee shoes before a crowd of 16,700 women. I wore them during the remainder of the evening, both onstage and at my book table. They continue to give me so much pleasure.

Many times God surprises me with gifts only after I've given away tangible resources of my own. On a recent Sunday morning I visited a New Creation Fellowship Church where an evangelist had been ministering for several days. I'd been praying during the week that God would clearly direct me to the person or organization He wanted me to give to next. While I was preparing to give my offering to the church that Sunday, my husband told me the amount he was writing his check for. It was a generous sum that ordinarily would have been sufficient for both of us. However, God spoke in my spirit again and told me to give the visiting evangelist $100 cash. I had it in my purse, but I didn't want to be without money. Giving away that $100 would almost wipe out my personal spending budget. However, I'd sold some books and had business funds, so I didn't really have an excuse for not parting with the bills. I dug around in my purse and came out with a $50 bill, thinking that should suffice. But again I sensed God's voice: "What did I tell you, Thelma?" *Okay, God!* I reached back into my purse, grabbed the other $50 bill, and walked up to the evangelist and handed it to her. I felt great!

Less than a week later I opened my mail, and there was a check for $100 from a dear friend who wanted me to have it for no particular reason. Wow! Once again God showed me that what I choose to do really does matter to Him, and He will honor my obedience. The safest place in the whole wide world is the center of God's will.

When someone gives you a gift of a smile, friendly handshake, card, object, or money, how do you feel? I feel happy, delighted, humble, and sometimes embarrassed. But I *always* feel blessed. I feel that the giver is wishing God's favor and goodness upon me. That is the blessing in receiving.

Prayer

Father, I realize that people don't have to give, so when they do, I know You're in it. They're following Your prompting, obeying Your direction. Thank You for using us to bless one another and for granting us the willingness to give without expecting anything in return. Help me be open to Your claim on all my resources so I can bless others in Your name. And thank You for all the surprises You have planned for me to receive. Amen.

God's Word to You

Give, and it will be given to you. A good measure, pressed down, shaken together and running over, will be poured into your lap. For with the measure you use, it will be measured to you (Luke 6:38).

Affirmation

As I give freely to others, I abundantly receive.

5

God Does the Drawing

I was going about my morning routine at the office some years ago when I had the idea to organize a women's retreat. My first thoughts were, *A women's retreat? I don't know anything about organizing a women's retreat. I don't have time to organize a women's retreat. I don't even want to organize a women's retreat. I can't conduct a women's retreat!*

But the notion kept invading my mind and tugging at my heart. When I spoke to my daughter Vikki and my assistant, Pat, about it, they thought it was a good idea. In fact, almost everything I suggested to them concerning speaking and possibly making money, they thought was a good idea.

Trying to figure out where to have the retreat and how much to charge and other details started to consume my thoughts. Then I remembered to pray! "Lord, You know I don't know what I'm doing. Give me some people or resources to help me, please." He did.

I recalled that I had met a woman on an airplane not many months earlier. She'd sent me a brochure of a company she worked for outside Flower Mound, Texas, called Circle R Ranch. I called her and scheduled an appointment to see the place. Then I thought of several energetic Christian women who were members of different churches in the Dallas–Fort Worth area and invited them to a meeting to create the format for the women's retreat. Over the weeks we prayed, fasted, and organized a retreat called "Becoming a Woman of Excellence." (At the time I hadn't heard of Cynthia Heald's bestselling Bible studies by the same name.)

We selected speakers, musicians, and volunteers, and one of the women who helped me plan offered to design and print the marketing brochures. I agreed. They were not going to be printed on slick, shiny paper, nor would they be in vivid colors. I had to settle for black and white. But they were free!

Then came the first hitch. One speaker involved in the program saw the brochures and was disturbed because they didn't look like the professional marketing pieces she and I were accustomed to. I think she was a little embarrassed to be promoted by such low-budget advertising. Because I respect her opinion very much, I agonized over what to do when she called with her concern. I wondered if other participants felt the same way but didn't want to hurt my feelings by telling me.

Confused about how to approach the situation and whether to discard the free brochures and spend money we really didn't have on classier ones, I closed the door of my office and prayed, "Lord, I don't know what to do. Things have been going along so smoothly until now. What am I supposed to do about these brochures? Help me, Lord!"

I finished praying and went about what I was doing in the office. Suddenly the Holy Spirit seemed to confirm to me, "Mere paper doesn't draw people to God. God does the drawing!"

What a relief! The burden of trying to redo those brochures was taken away. Then my task was to tell the worried participant my decision and allow her to decide whether she wanted to still take part in the retreat. I prayed again and asked God to give me wisdom in talking with her. He did.

I told her about praying and what I felt the Holy Spirit was telling me. She had the choice of accepting or rejecting what I said. Since she is a gracious woman of God and a good friend, she said, "Okay, it's up to you, Thelma. It's your program. I'll be there." And she made a tremendous contribution to the success of the retreat!

It's funny how we sometimes let little things that really don't matter become big problems. We need to keep in mind that whatever God ordains, He sustains. I needed to remember that the idea of the retreat wasn't mine—it was God's. God already had the speakers, musicians, and volunteers picked out, as well as the person who was going to be in charge of the brochures. All I needed to do was follow His plan. It was laid out perfectly and completely.

I'd been shortsighted when I'd asked God for 40 women to attend the retreat. He drew 150 women from all over the state of Texas! On that day, women were healed from sicknesses and restored to emotional and spiritual health. Families were put back together, and participants found renewed confidence as women of God. We shared our dreams and spent private time with the Lord. Several women told me that things happened in their hearts that changed their lives for the better. I don't know all that happened, but God does. After all, He did the drawing.

Just think, I'd almost let a humble black-and-white brochure hinder the progress of what God had planned. I'd also tried to talk myself out of doing what God had clearly told me to do. If I had, I would have aborted God's wonderful plans to let me be a part of His healing and delivering many people that day.

Thank God that He is bigger than our hesitations, fears, and pride! When we obey His directions, He works miracles through us—and even in spite of us. Hallelujah!

Prayer

Lord, I often ask You to guide me and reveal Your plans for me, but sometimes when You do, I foolishly try to get away with not doing what You tell me. Thank You for being patient and persistent with me. Thank You for trusting me enough to give me projects when You know I don't know how to do them. Thank You for always being faithful to provide the mechanisms that bring about success. You are the kind and gentle Designer of my life. Keep me ever in Your will and in Your ways. Amen.

God's Word to You

May the favor of the Lord our God rest upon us; establish the work of our hands for us—yes, establish the work of our hands (Psalm 90:17).

Affirmation

God's favor makes whatever I do for Him successful.

6

Divine Awakenings

I often wonder why God wakes me up in the wee hours of the morning and puts ideas in my head. Is it because everybody else is asleep and He knows I won't be distracted? Is it because He knows that's the time I'm most receptive? Regardless, invariably He'll wake me up between three and five o'clock.

I wrote the credo for the Bumblebee Club, a group of supporters of my former television program, around three thirty.

I wrote the business plan for my company in the early morning hours.

I pray for people before daybreak.

I meditate with God long before I do anything else.

Some of my most creative time is between three and six in the morning. I'm awakened sometimes with groaning and travail from the bottom of my being. I've been warned of impending danger. I've known when some of my relatives died. One morning I had a dream that my husband's Aunt Essie was in a casket in the front of our church, but she was sitting straight up and preaching. Immediately after that dream, God woke me up and confirmed in my spirit that Essie was dead. When my husband woke up later that morning, I told him what had happened. Almost as soon as I finished telling him, the telephone rang. Aunt Doretha, Essie's sister, told us Essie had died that morning.

The dream about the casket had appeared to me before. Several weeks before Granny died, Mrs. Fay Pruitt, one of Granny's deceased friends, appeared to me as I saw Granny lying in a casket in front of the church. Mrs. Pruitt said, "Mrs. Harrell's coming, and it won't be long now." Immediately God woke me up. I knew Granny would die soon. My "death dreams" may sound morbid, but each time there was a calmness about the dream that kept me from feeling frightened or upset.

I believe God talks to us. Have I ever heard God speak to me in an audible voice? No. Yes, some people say that's how He talks to them. Other people say they feel Him inside their spirit. God speaks to me in a variety of ways. Sometimes it's through dreams as I sleep and visions as I meditate. I can tell if it's God speaking to me because I can remember all the details of the dream or vision as if I had just dreamed it.

Sometimes my left ear gets numb as He speaks in my mind.

Sometimes He speaks to me through Scripture. Sometimes He speaks to me...

- through the words of a song

- through a reading or a sermon

- through a quote or a prayer

- through a word of advice or admonition

- through the honesty of a child

- through a billboard or bumper sticker

- through a conversation with a family member or friend

When He wakes me up in the wee hours of the morning, He has my complete and undivided attention.

- When He speaks to me, He is never frightening.

- He never tells me to do something that is harmful to me or someone else.

- He always tells me things that are in line with His holy Word.

- He doesn't always give me all the details.

- His information is always correct.

- When I follow His directions, I make no mistakes.

- He brings to pass everything He says.

I'm amazed and humbled to realize that an awesome, omnipotent, sovereign God wants to communicate with me. That's one of the reasons He created people: He wants us to fellowship with Him. Many people have tried to explain how to hear the voice of God. In my opinion, nobody has been able to describe it fully. I believe God's sheep know the Shepherd's voice by faith.

If you want to hear what God has to say to you, simply ask Him. In the Lord's Prayer, Jesus said to pray to God and include these requests:

- "Your will be done on earth as it is in heaven" (Matthew 6:10).

- "Lead us not into temptation but deliver us from the evil one" (verse 13).

These requests open the door for God to personally communicate with you. Heed the voice of the Master!

Prayer

God, You are the Master at getting Your children's attention. Thank You for the unique ways You communicate with me. Please give me ears to clearly hear what You tell me and the strength and courage to follow through. Many things wouldn't be accomplished without Your guidance. Thank You for always being here to let me know which way to go. Amen.

God's Word to You

Whether you turn to the right or to the left, your ears will hear a voice behind you, saying, "This is the way; walk in it" (Isaiah 30:21).

Affirmation

God always communicates clearly to me when I listen.

7

Anger Is Not a Virtue

I will never forget that October night when I deplaned at Washington DC on my way to Indian Head, Maryland, for a speaking engagement. The weather was pleasant outside, but my thoughts were tossing and turning. I'd been informed earlier in the day that in Indian Head everything shut down in the early evening. The motel closed at ten o'clock. Out of sympathy, the woman manager had agreed to stay there until midnight. If I didn't get there before then, I wouldn't have a place to stay. I'd be on my own.

The five o'clock flight from Houston to Washington was delayed more than two hours. We'd sat on the runway in Houston all that time—long enough for the whirlwind in my head to start. *What if I get to Indian Head and the woman is gone? What if I don't get there at all tonight? I have to speak at eight o'clock in the morning. What if my commute to Indian Head takes longer than I expect? What if the car rental counter is closed when I get there? What are my options?*

While my mind imagined various catastrophes, I developed a plan. *When I get off the plane, I will have my driver's license and confirmation number readily available for the car rental clerk. He or she will have empathy for me and will get me out of there quickly and efficiently.* I had it all figured out—I thought.

I dashed off the plane and proceeded directly to the car rental counter, prepared with all the identification needed to make it a quick and easy transaction. My plan didn't work. The clerk had tunnel vision. I offered her my driver's license and confirmation number and asked her to enter them in the computer so the profile would give her instructions concerning the car. Her response was, "I need to see your credit card." I replied, "Ma'am, if you will input my confirmation number, everything will show up in my profile, including my credit card information."

"I said, I need to see your credit card!" she demanded.

"Trust me," I answered. "If you will put the information into your computer, you will see what to do. This is an unusual situation, ma'am. I need to get to Indian Head, Maryland, before midnight." It was eleven thirty.

With an indignant tone of voice, the clerk exclaimed, "You must not have heard what I said. I need to see your credit card!"

That did it! I lost my cool. I screeched, "Woman, you'd better put in my confirmation number if you know what's good for you! I'm going to Indian Head tonight if I have to take you with me." (I didn't realize until I left the counter that I was threatening to kidnap that woman.) I continued, "If you don't know what to do in unusual situations, ask somebody. Don't just tell me you need my credit card. If you would do what I said, you'd discover that the car rental is billed directly to the company I'm working for."

I continued my tirade until a young man came out of another area and asked what was going on. (He heard me shouting, no doubt.) My gracious response to him was, "And who are you?" He told me he was the manager. Oh boy, did I let him have it. I told him that he should be training people to understand and handle unusual situations, that as tired as travelers are at the end of a day, especially after waiting on a plane for more than two hours before takeoff, his clerks should be ready, willing, and able to give the most excellent customer service possible, which included listening to the customers.

He was so nice, and he agreed with me. I'd become so irate that I didn't even notice he'd taken my driver's license and confirmation number from me, put them into the computer, and presented me with car keys. He got my attention when he said the documents were in order, the car was ready, and he'd be happy to escort me to the vehicle.

Well, I wasn't finished. With my hands on my hips and my eyebrows raised, I proclaimed angrily, "And, anyway, do you know who I am? My name is Thelma Wells. I teach customer service all over the world." My eyes boring through the female clerk, I continued, "I teach people how not to get upset when they deal with people like you."

Yes, I was downright ugly that night.

When I eventually got to Indian Head (much past midnight), there was no one to meet me. The only place to stay in the small town was a no-name motel that was then closed. I'd have to bunk down in the car for the night. Around two o'clock a woman came out of one of the rooms to get a soft drink. I asked her for a blanket because it was cold. She declined. I also asked her if there was anyplace else I could get some rest. My body was aching from trying to get comfortable in the car. She told me to go to the first signal light and make a right. I did. I drove and drove, endlessly it seemed, down dark, winding roads. It was so dark I thought Big Foot would walk out of the forest any minute!

Just beyond a massive grove of trees I spotted a Shell service station sign. The most beautiful sign I'd ever seen because it indicated civilization was near. As I got to the intersection where the gas station was, I looked to my left and saw another beautiful sign: Motel 8. Swiftly I turned into the entrance, shuffled painfully to the office, and pounded on the door to get the desk clerk's attention. The woman was compassionate. Even though the motel was closed, she invited me in and comforted me while I told her about my ordeal. I thanked God that I finally had a resting place, even if only for one hour. It seemed like the fastest hour in my sleep history.

Five o'clock came too soon. Time to arise and make that 45-minute trip from La Plata, Maryland, to Indian Head. I had to get back in time to stand in line with the construction workers and other contractors for a pass to enter the naval base where I was going to be teaching.

Miraculously the day went well. Four o'clock came quickly, and I was off to Washington DC and the infamous car rental counter. I had more than an hour's drive to think about the previous day and how I'd responded. I wasn't proud of myself. As a "customer service and how-to-deal-with-difficult-people" trainer, I had not done a good job of walking my talk. I'd lost perspective on who I was and whose I was. I'd allowed myself to act totally in the flesh.

When I'd asked the people at the car rental counter if they knew who I was, that question should have been directed to me! "Thelma, do you know who you are? Do you know who you are representing everywhere you go? Do you think Christ would act the way you are? Do you think the Lord is proud of your conduct? Do you have a repentant heart for the way you acted? Thelma, as a Christian, what are you going to do when you get back to the car rental agency?"

I walked up to the counter. The woman who provoked me was standing with her back to me as she faced the computer. I spoke to her. She looked around, saw me, and then immediately turned back to the computer. I spoke to her again in a pleading voice, attempting to communicate how sorry I was for the way I'd acted. Without turning to me, she shook her head. She wouldn't let me apologize.

I've reflected on that situation for many years. I've concluded that the clerk didn't, in fact, "make" me mad. I responded to her based on the storm that was raging within me. I felt totally at the clerk's mercy. When I felt I had no control, I fell apart and made a spectacle of myself.

As Christians, how often do we operate totally in the flesh and allow our jumbled thoughts and emotions to dictate our conduct? When I rushed into the airport rental agency, I'd already set the stage for that unsettling interaction. The "what ifs" had me, and I wasn't going to be taken alive! So I worried and schemed. I don't remember asking God to take charge of the situation and have His way in it. I don't remember asking for protection and grace. I don't remember asking Him to give me peace in the middle of the storm.

The fact is, when we take charge of situations without consulting the wisdom of God, we always make messes of them. Relationships get convoluted, hearts get broken, unfair and unkind words are spoken, egos are crushed, waves of doubt trouble us, distrust creeps in, guilt takes up residence, and emotions go haywire. "Thangs ain't pretty."

Think of the times you've become angry or out of control. What was happening? Did you feel safe and secure? Did you feel competent and confident? Did you have faith that God was in perfect control of your life? I don't think so.

What do you think would happen in our lives if we maintained an attitude of prayer in *every* situation? What might have happened had I not attempted to manipulate the situation at the car rental desk? I believe I would have left there in time to make it to Indian Head before midnight. I know I wouldn't have been hostile and belligerent. And I would have been able to return to that rental desk with a clear conscience. I certainly would have had more of a mind to thank God for His favor and protection on the trip.

Thank God because He never gives up on remaking us in His image! No matter how obnoxious our behavior can be at times, He is willing to convict and correct us so we can become more like Him.

Prayer

Lord, thank You for giving me all the ammunition I need to hold back the enemy of anger. Too often I take that strong emotion and use it against Your will in order to accomplish my will. How often I stumble and make a mess! I take charge, talk out of turn, and refuse to listen to You. Too often I already have my mind made up about how things should be. Your Word says You are gracious, full of compassion, slow to anger, and possess great mercy. By the power of the Holy Spirit, please conform me to Your image. Amen.

God's Word to You

And we, who with unveiled faces all reflect the Lord's glory, are being transformed into his likeness with ever-increasing glory, which comes from the Lord, who is the Spirit (2 Corinthians 3:18).

Affirmation

Because of the Holy Spirit's transforming work within me,
I will put aside my natural self-interest
and behave more like Jesus.

8

God's Miraculous Signs

A funny thing happened to me in Colorado Springs one year. I was there for an important meeting with people who helped make me look good back then—my literary agent, Kathy, and my editor, Traci. The scenery was beautiful. The afternoon rain was gentle. The temperature was just right. Even though the tip of Pikes Peak was surrounded by pillows of white clouds and I couldn't see the whole mountain, just looking at that world wonder and seeing the foothills round about were spectacular. I had the pleasure of meeting new people, eating good food, and working in a comfortable, homey environment all afternoon. I had no idea I'd be rewarded with two extraordinary surprises near the end of the day.

Since I was a very young girl, I've believed that if you want to know whether or not something's right for you, you need to ask God for a sign. I must have picked up the idea from hearing about God's giving signs of His favor or disfavor to people in the Bible. For example, when I was 14 years old, I asked God to give me a sign when I met the man I was going to marry. Sure, I was too young to be thinking about getting married, but people always told me I was "old for my age." Anyway, I told God that when He wanted to show me who I was going to marry, I'd consider it a sign from Him if everything I did within one day was related to cleanliness. For instance, let me clean the house, change the sheets, shampoo my hair, take a bath, and do everything "clean" in one day. "Weird!" you say? Well, the sign made sense to me. When I was a young girl, we didn't have hot running water. We had to boil water to wash clothes, and we did that only on Mondays. Most black folks didn't shampoo their hair more than every two weeks back then, and in Granny's house that was done on Saturdays. Other days of the week were designated for bathing, washing dishes, and so forth. To do all the "clean" things on one day would have been extremely unusual in our household.

I met my husband before I turned 15, even though we didn't marry until I was 20. One Saturday God gave me the custom-made sign I'd asked for. I got up early and changed the linens on the bed and washed clothes in the bathtub, I cleaned and mopped the kitchen, I dusted and swept the house, I raked the leaves off the grass and swept the porch, I went to the beauty shop for a shampoo, and I bathed that night. In Sunday school the next day I looked at George Wells for the first time. I said to myself, *I'm gonna marry dat boy!* I was convinced that this shy, seemingly quiet, handsome, skinny country boy was the husband God had assigned to me. All these years later, I'm still convinced of that!

Before I went to Colorado Springs to talk about the next book I was planning to write, I'd asked God for a confirming sign. I wasn't specific; I just asked Him to show me somehow, in a specific way I'd recognize, that I was following His perfect will. As Kathy drove me to the airport after our meeting that afternoon, the sky filled with the most gorgeous, awesome sight. Directly ahead of us were two rainbows. They looked like huge handles on the largest Easter basket in the universe. The aqua, yellow, orange, red, and purple bands were so brilliant they seemed to have spotlights illuminating them from behind.

I mentioned to Kathy that rainbows were significant in my life. I had asked God more than once to give me a rainbow during a very trying time to let me know that my personal storm was passing over and everything would work out all right. He'd shown me rainbows on three occasions. The double rainbow in Colorado Springs meant a lot to me. I had never seen anything like that before, and I fully believe God was telling me I was on the right track with the book I was writing. This was an assignment from Him.

But that's not all that happened that August day. I flew home on American Airlines and was assigned seat number 5E. The person assigned to the seat by the window entered the plane with his wife. When I noticed that his wife was assigned to the row in front of us, I asked him if he wanted to sit with her. If so, I would gladly exchange seats with her. They were happy!

I was in my new seat, when a young man sat beside me. I was so sleepy, I didn't really pay any attention to him until we were well on our way. He looked up at me from the book he was reading and got my attention. He said, "I know who you are." I thought, *He must have read one of my books or heard me speak. Finally somebody's noticing me!* (Okay, maybe I was just a little full of myself for a moment.)

"Your name is Thelma Wells," he continued. "You were my first boss when I was 17 years old. Do you remember me? My name is Randy Edwards."

Randy? Randy Edwards? I thought. *NorthPark Bank, maybe?*

Randy continued, "I remember your face. But I really recognized you by your ring. I always thought that was the prettiest ring. Mrs. Wells, you haven't changed a bit. You are so special to me. Do you remember that you made me go to school? I took banking classes because of you. Now I have a degree in finance and work in many parts of the world as a financial adviser in real estate."

My chest puffed up to a size 60. I was a proud puppy! *Just look at this young man,* I thought. *I had something to do with his success.* He didn't make my head any smaller when he announced to his wife and her friend, loud enough for all of first class to hear, "Look, Honey, this lady was my first boss and made me go to banking school. Isn't this cool? My very first boss when I was 17!" Randy put the finishing touches on an already unforgettable day.

If I hadn't gotten up and given that woman a seat next to her husband, I might never have gotten to see Randy. I took that as a sign that the good we do for others will come back to bless us. Randy sure blessed me!

According to *Strong's Concordance,* a sign is "an unusual occurrence, transcending the common course of nature." Some signs portend a remarkable event soon to happen. Others are miracles and wonders by which God authenticates the people sent by Him, or by which people prove that the cause they are pleading is God's.

I believe God gives signs to all of us, even when we don't ask for them. But God doesn't always deliver the signs we ask for. When He doesn't, that too is a sign to heed. Often when I'm getting ready to make serious decisions, I ask for a specific sign to signal whether or not to go forward with what I think I want. For instance, when I was trying to make a decision about continuing my television show, I asked God for three signs within a certain time frame. I had to make my decision quickly. When God didn't deliver any of the three things I asked Him for, I took that as a signal to table the television show for whatever else God had in store for me. I had no idea what would come next. I accepted God's nondelivery by faith. The time was right to end the show, and I did so. I accept all signs by faith because God doesn't let me in on all the details about anything I'm contemplating.

Maybe you've asked God for a sign or for some evidence that He's working in your life. Many of the people in the Bible took signs seriously, and I think we should too. Just read Judges 6:17; 2 Kings 20:9; Isaiah 7:14; 38:7; John 20:29-31 for a few references to how God has used signs throughout the ages. Maybe you'd like to add this method to your ways of communicating with God. You might be amazed!

Prayer

Father, You have used signs for generations to let people know what You want them to do. When I'm making decisions or need something confirmed, You understand my humanness, and You've often graciously met my need for a tangible sign that I'm headed in the right direction. When You don't give me an obvious sign, You give me Your peace instead. Thank You for being a God I can trust. Amen.

God's Word to You

"This is the LORD's sign to you that the LORD will do what he has promised: I will make the shadow cast by the sun go back the ten steps it has gone down on the stairway of Ahaz." So the sunlight went back the ten steps it had gone down (Isaiah 38:7-8).

Affirmation

I am confident about my direction when I see signs of God's favor and experience His peace.

9

Did I Have to
Get Burned to Listen?

George and I had a wonderful Fourth of July. Our children, their spouses, our grandchildren, and other relatives gathered at our home to eat fried shrimp, mashed potatoes, catfish, hush puppies, potato salad, lemonade, and ice cream. It was so good!

After everyone left, I had a serious craving for more shrimp so I fixed some for George and me. We ate and reminisced about the day's activities. It had been a perfect day—talking, laughing, and enjoying our family. I rose to clean the kitchen before spending the rest of the evening with my honey. The grease from the deep fryer was still hot. Because I didn't want to wait until it cooled, I lifted the deep fryer and started pouring the grease into a plastic storage container. Well, you can imagine what happened next. The plastic container immediately melted, and I dropped the deep fryer. Hot grease splashed all over my right arm and hand.

"Oh mercy!" I yelled. "I'm on fire! Don't panic...don't panic! Get ice water...get the medical book...call 911! Do something!" My mind was in a whirlwind. My husband rushed me to the emergency room. I was treated for second- and third-degree burns. I was released from the hospital, but they didn't tell me I should rest to give my body a chance to heal. And even if I had been told to rest, I probably wouldn't have. I had too much to do. Yes, the pain was excruciating, but I was scheduled to speak at a conference the next day. And for months my daughter, my grandson, and I had been planning to attend the National Speakers Association's annual convention the following week. I was also scheduled to sing with an ensemble at the convention and participate on a panel. I had to be there! I'd given my word.

By the time I arrived at the convention, I was exhausted. In fact, I was too tired to move. I tried to get out of bed but couldn't. My head was spinning, my arm was hurting, my stomach was rolling, my body was aching. I was sick! My immune system had shut down. I foolishly forced myself to keep my obligations because I was intent on keeping my word. And besides, I figured that's what God would want (but I didn't ask Him).

I became more ill. The doctor at a local clinic informed me that I had a 104-degree temperature and gastritis. "Go home," he said. "Take these antibiotics. Drink plenty of water. Get some rest!" I finally did. I had no choice.

Three days later, at 3:19 in the morning, God woke me up. I sat up in bed listening. I couldn't do much more. In the stillness I heard God in my spirit. I knew He was telling me that my life was taking a new direction. Certain paths had come to an end, and new trails were emerging. Finally God had my undivided attention. It had been too long since I'd really stopped to ask Him what He wanted me to be doing. I'd been too busy forging ahead on my own agenda. God used my sickness and my need for rest as an opportunity to get me to listen to Him. I'm sure He tried to communicate with me earlier, but I was just too harried to hear Him.

You don't have to learn the hard way like I did. You don't have to get burned or injured before you slow down and listen to God. Stop and listen to God every day. Quiet your spirit before Him, and ask Him to communicate with You. God has plenty to say to you if you'll give Him your attention. Psalm 46:10 tells us we will know God and His sovereignty when we are "still." So be still and know His will for you.

Prayer

Father, You know all I've promised to do. What with home, church, social activities, and other responsibilities, I barely have time to breathe. Help me to slow down. Help me to "just say no" sometimes. I know You desire and deserve my time. I depend on Your guidance. I want to hear from You today. And remind me often to stop, listen, and wait on You. Amen.

God's Word to You

This is what the Sovereign LORD, the Holy One of Israel, says: "In repentance and rest is your salvation, in quietness and trust is your strength, but you would have none of it... Yet the LORD longs to be gracious to you; he rises to show you compassion. For the LORD is a God of justice. Blessed are all who wait for him!" (Isaiah 30:15,18).

Affirmation

When I slow down and spend quality time with God,
He reveals Himself to me.

10

When God Says No

For four years I was a part of the Business Incubation Center in Dallas and leased an office in that wing of the Bill J. Priest Center. Abruptly I was asked to leave because I'd graduated from the business training program. *Well, what am I supposed to do now?* I huffed to myself.

My resourceful assistant (and daughter) found a wonderful building with ample office space in a prestigious area near downtown Dallas. To our amazement, the leasing price was just right. The lovely 42-year-old, off-white brick, two-story landmark on Fairmount was an answer to two prayers. First I'd prayed for a convenient office location with enough working space for the machines and personnel. I'd planned in my mind the office building I was going to have built and how I was going to decorate it. The desire of my heart was to be the proud owner of an office building with my name on the cornerstone and a sign in front with gold letters: THELMA WELLS AND ASSOCIATES. When we found this building, I abandoned my building plans because leasing this space was perfect…and I dreamed of eventually buying it.

The building's owner lived upstairs in a lovely apartment with a beautiful picture window in the living room overlooking the front of the building. A large den, a modern kitchen, a pantry, two bedrooms, and two baths completed the apartment. There was even a deck in back. I envisioned holding seminars and mini-retreats there. I daydreamed about that space all the time.

About a year after we moved into the office space, the owner died. His daughter put the building up for sale. She didn't list it because I'd made it known I wanted to buy the place. I loved it. It was comfortable, convenient, and reasonably priced. I knew God wanted me to have this building. I'd been praying to own it for a long time.

But I was in for a rude awakening. I didn't know that people over 50 years of age, self-employed, and without accounts receivable were considered poor risks for a 30-year mortgage. My friends in the banking industry all but told me to forget about it. I huffed and puffed for days because nobody would finance the loan for the building. By the time I'd made my rounds of the local bankers, the building owner had hired a Realtor, and people had started coming by to look at the property. I was cordial, but I still thought God was going to give me that building. After all, He knew how much I wanted it!

Time went on and nothing changed. Finally a Realtor purchased the building and moved into the lovely apartment upstairs. I thought, *Hey, wait a minute!* But God knew what He was doing! I was scheduled to speak at several New Life Women of Faith Joyful Journey conferences in several cities, but I didn't know that within a month I'd be asked to become a permanent part of the group's plans. God was on top of my situation! He'd already planned for me to be debt-free with no concerns about having to maintain business property. The plans He had for me didn't include giving seminars in that upstairs apartment. God knew I'd be on the road ministering to many hurting women in the United States and elsewhere. He knew that owning an office building would have been a burden, so it wasn't His perfect will for me.

I love the promise in Psalm 37:23: "The steps of a good [woman] are ordered by the LORD" (NKJV). My constant prayer for the past several years had been that God would close doors He didn't want me to walk through and open doors where He wanted me to go. I asked Him to keep me from wasting precious time. In His faithfulness, sometimes He said no to my passionate requests.

As I've studied what Scripture has to say about prayer, I've discovered these truths:

- God answers all prayers.
- Sometimes He answers them immediately.

- Sometimes He delays.

- Sometimes He says no.

- Sometimes His answer is a surprise.

God answers our prayers not according to our wishes, but according to His perfect will. Hallelujah!

Another thing I discovered is that when God says no, He gives us incomprehensible peace, which validates that His no is right on. Once I've accepted His no answers, He replaces what I thought I wanted with something even better! I'm glad He saved me from the headache of that building. He had so much more planned for me than I ever imagined. And now the new owner is having to do costly repairs.

Several years ago I went through a similar process when I tried to buy a house. Nothing was working out the way I'd expected. I got angry at the people and a little upset with God because I thought I knew what was best. In the end, again, I got far better than what I was aiming for. I ended up in a bigger, better constructed house for half the cost.

Then there was the car I wanted. A Mercedes-Benz. But it was a status symbol God knew I didn't really need. My ego needed adjusting...so God did it. Once I was cured from that, He gave me a car I love with a monthly payment that doesn't make me sick every time I write the check.

Not being able to plan or predict my future doesn't bother me anymore. God does such a great job, so why should I try to usurp His authority? Now I just ask Him for what I think I want and wait for His confirmation on whether it's a good thing or not. I leave everything up to Him. This sure relieves me of a lot of burdens! When I committed my life to Him, I told Him I wanted Him to be the Lord and Master over me and all He entrusts to me. And if I really meant it, I shouldn't have a problem letting Him take charge. "Let go and let God" means a lot to me. The Thelma Wells version says, "Stop thinking you're running something when you ain't." God's got my life under control. Whew!

Prayer

Father, I know You have my whole life under Your loving control.
You know what I need, how much I need, and when to intervene

and save me from things I have no business with. Sometimes I object to Your answers to my prayers, but to tell You the truth, I'm glad You take charge. Keep showing me Your skill in caring for my future. Keep teaching me to wait on You. Keep guiding me along Your path. Thank You for giving me Your peace even when You tell me no. Amen.

God's Word to You

May the God of peace, who through the blood of the eternal covenant brought back from the dead our Lord Jesus, that great Shepherd of the sheep, equip you with everything good for doing his will, and may he work in us what is pleasing to him, through Jesus Christ, to whom be glory for ever and ever. Amen (Hebrews 13:20-21).

Affirmation

When God says no, I have the opportunity to trust Him even more.

11

I Thought I Knew
What I Was Doing

I don't like going to meetings. I'd always found little value in the meetings of the organizations I was affiliated with. So when Dennis McCuistion invited me to become a member of the North Texas Speakers Association (NTSA), I wasn't interested. He kept telling me I was missing a great opportunity to improve my speaking business, but I decided I was already a successful speaker, so what could NTSA offer me? And it would require a time commitment I didn't want to make.

Dennis and I met when we were both teaching for the Dallas chapter of the American Institute of Banking. We got better acquainted when we became members of the board of directors of that banking organization. Eventually Dennis and I became professional speakers. He'd gotten involved in the North Texas Speakers Association and the National Speakers Association (NSA) and realized the value of these organizations. Because my business was thriving, I really thought I knew everything there was to know about what I was doing. Each time Dennis called to invite me to an NTSA meeting, I had an excuse to not go. But Dennis was his usual persistent self and wouldn't take no for an answer. Finally I agreed to attend one meeting to get him off my back.

That Saturday morning meeting was truly an eye-opening, humbling experience. I learned more about the business of speaking than I could have learned in five years of running a business. I suddenly became keenly aware that professional speaking was actually a career for me—no longer just a hobby. If I were going to continue to succeed in this business, I'd better get organized, keep up-to-date documentation, and do a more professional job of contracting with my customers. I thought I was doing things very well, but I wasn't.

One other important fact stood out to me: The people in the NTSA organization were willing and happy to share information and help guide others in the right direction. I didn't know anyone there personally except Dennis, yet those people were willing to help me become a better professional speaker. *Wow! What a giving group!* I thought. *I think I'm going to like this.*

The group leaders announced that the National Speakers Association was sponsoring an upcoming workshop in San Antonio. I decided then and there to attend. The local chapter seemed too good to be true, so perhaps the real scoop about this organization would be revealed at the San Antonio meeting. When I went, I discovered the truth sure enough. The organization and its people were indeed very caring and giving. The workshops were full of information that I could put to use immediately. I was convinced. This was the organization for me!

In June I received a telephone call from the NSA informing me that I'd been selected to present a showcase (an 8-minute keynote speech) at the NSA convention in Phoenix the following month. "Me? Speak for the National Speakers Association?" I asked. The caller assured me she had the right person. Dennis' wife, Nikki, had sent my brochure and a recording to the NSA national office. There was one little hitch though: Speakers were required to be members of the NSA, and I was not. "Ma'am, how much is the membership fee?" I asked. She told me, and I promptly wrote the check and sent it by overnight mail. I was an official member and going to speak at the convention! I couldn't believe it!

The knowledge I gained from this group tremendously enhanced my career. The day I presented my showcase, one of the owners of CareerTrack was in the audience. Within a month, I was traveling and teaching for them. They were a national seminar company that contracts with professional speakers to teach business courses throughout the world. Soon I was in a more prominent position in the professional speaking arena. My visibility increased in industries I hadn't previously penetrated, and I gained credibility because of my association with professional speaking organizations. The peak of my NSA activities was when I was asked to deliver a keynote address in a general session at the Dallas national convention. It was the first time in the history of the NSA that a black woman was center stage before the entire convention.

And just think…I would have missed the eventful occasion if I hadn't finally listened to Dennis and attended an NTSA meeting. From that point on I've learned to never say "never." As determined as I was *not* to join another organization that meets regularly, by getting involved I estimate that I cut my business learning curve time by five years. God uses many methods to prepare us for the tasks He assigns. Increasing our knowledge isn't always confined to the Bible, but it is confirmed by it. Being open to learning from different sources is a sign of great wisdom.

Prayer

God, I don't know everything about anything. Thank You for the obvious and the unexpected opportunities You give me to increase my knowledge so I can serve You better. Help me continue to want and seek knowledge. Amen.

God's Word to You

I have filled him with the Spirit of God, with skill, ability and knowledge in all kinds of crafts (Exodus 31:3).

Affirmation

I embrace the opportunity to learn something new every day.

12

It's Time to Go

Contemplating whether or not to quit my banking job and go into business for myself was a frightening dilemma. I was hired at the Republic National Bank in Dallas as a proof operator. I reconciled big corporate accounts. At the bank, mothers were allowed to come to work at ten and leave at two, which fit well with my children's schedule. But I realized soon after starting the job that it wasn't my life's calling. I started praying that God would give me a job where I could feel much greater satisfaction and where I could move up and have some authority to use my innate leadership ability.

I was determined to get a better job, and NorthPark National Bank was my target. My husband and I banked there, it was near our home, and it was a pretty place to be all day. I called the personnel director and asked him to meet me at the door of the bank at closing time. With some objections that I didn't accept, he reluctantly met me and accepted my resume. The challenge was on!

Several times a week I called to ask for an interview. He kept telling me there were no jobs available. I kept telling him there would be a job opening, and I wanted it. Several weeks passed before the personnel director finally called me in for a general interview (probably just to get me off his back). Then there was yet another wait. Impatiently and persistently I called the bank until one day there was an opening in the New Accounts Department, and I was invited in for a serious interview. I finally became a member of the NorthPark National Bank staff! Mind you, I knew absolutely nothing about banking. Running a proof machine hadn't prepared me in the least.

I worked hard and moved up rapidly at NorthPark, from the position of new accounts clerk to customer service supervisor to banking officer to assistant vice president. Within three years I had also become an instructor for the American Institute of Banking in Dallas, Fort Worth, Houston, Austin, Chicago, and Minneapolis, as well as a trainer for the Bank Administration Institutes throughout the state of Texas. In some Texas banking circles I was described as "the last word in new accounts." That's because an attorney and I had written a new accounts manual that outlined in detail all the legalities and methods of opening and maintaining new accounts documents in Texas. The manual was distributed throughout the state, and I received plenty of accolades for my contribution.

While teaching banking classes, I developed a short seminar about how people could become the best of whatever they wanted to be. Students in my classes began asking me to come to their banks, business organizations, club meetings, churches, and all sorts of other places to deliver that motivational speech. At the same time, people were inviting me to conduct training sessions on subjects I didn't know anything about. Someone would call and ask me if I taught telephone skills. "Of course!" I'd reply. I needed the business, and I was willing and able to learn. Once a group was serious about hiring me to speak, I spent hours, including many sleepless nights, developing a seminar on that subject.

Although I was highly successful in banking, I began contemplating leaving and becoming an entrepreneur by going into professional speaking full-time. I discussed my idea with my husband and asked for his blessing, but he didn't believe it was God's timing. There was no way I would go into business without my husband's full support. I considered his discomfort a clue about God's will, so I asked God to let my husband be in total agreement when the time was right. Two years later my family and I spent one of the most wonderful vacations of our lives in Montego Bay, Jamaica. As we were flying home from vacation, I knew in my heart that it would soon be time for me to confer with George again about changing jobs.

Going back to work was much more stressful than preparing for vacation. I sensed that something was about to change severely. My boss welcomed me back from vacation with a conversation concerning the direction he saw for the work I had done on the new accounts manual and other training products for the banking industry. He suggested that I allow the bank to market the products under the bank's name, and I would receive a small commission on what was sold. Because the material wasn't written just for my bank or during work hours…and it was being distributed throughout the state, that didn't sound like a good business deal to me. The passion for going into business for myself was getting stronger! But so was the fear of leaving my secure position.

When lunchtime came, I collected my purse, several sharpened pencils, and a legal-size yellow writing pad. I headed for Wyatt's Cafeteria in the NorthPark Mall.

"Lord, give me wisdom," I prayed. "I've got to really think about what I'm going to do." I had read somewhere that Dr. Viktor Frankl developed a method of dealing with fear called paradoxical intention. I recalled the method and used it to help determine what the next step in my decision process should be. I…

- wrote down the situation. I needed to determine whether or not to leave my banking job and start a full-time professional speaking business.

- wrote down all the advantages and disadvantages. I made a list of all the pros and cons I could think of for leaving my job and for going into business for myself.

- determined the worst-case scenario. What was the worst thing I could expect to happen if I left the bank and started my own business?

- asked, "What difference will it make?" As I reviewed all my pros and cons, I asked myself how important they would be in the next one to five years.

The last question helped me decide that it was indeed time to ask my husband again for his support. How would I ever know whether or not I could make it in business if I never tried? At that point I penned a new definition of failure: Failure is never trying to do what is in your heart. Psalm 37 reminds us that when we live for God and want to be in His perfect will, He places desires in our hearts that are designed to help us carry out His will more fully. I was convinced He had placed the desire for my own business deep within my heart.

Excited but nervous, I waited for the right time to approach George.

Once I told him about the offer my boss had made, he felt the same sinking feeling about it I had. His emphatic response? "It's time to go out on your own! If you don't do it now, you're going to do it later. Go for it now."

Then I got really scared. My dream was becoming reality. It was time to tell my boss that instead of allowing the bank to exploit my handiwork, I was going to quit. Writing my resignation wasn't easy. After working at the bank for more than ten years, I had status, authority, a paycheck, insurance, and other perks. *What in the world was I doing?* But the passion of my heart to be a professional speaker spoke louder than my fear. I'd known for some time that what I really wanted out of life was to travel globally, extracting diamonds out of people's dust. I wanted to help people be better people. It was time to go!

Just to make sure, I sought the opinion of someone who loved the Lord, lived for Him, and would give me her honest perspective on my thinking process. I called George's Aunt Doretha Cashaw and told her I had something urgent to talk with her about. She came by our house that evening, and I told her of my decision to resign from the bank and start a speaking business. She asked me if I'd talked to the Lord and my husband about it. When I answered yes, she gave the best philosophical/theological thesis of anyone I'd paid attention to in a long time. She said, "If God said do it, you do it. What God ordains, He sustains. Step on out there in faith, Baby. Everything we do is in faith whether we know it or not. What do you have to lose if you're doing it for God and He gets the glory?"

Much to my boss' dismay, I resigned. Three days later I walked back into that bank as a training consultant and got my very first large contract to continue training people for the bank until the end of the year. God financed my business without my having to borrow a single penny. What a mighty God we serve!

Are you facing a frightening decision in an area of your life? Be assured that God knows all about the situation. He also has a solution for you. Ask Him for wisdom. Ask Him to show you what He wants you to do. Trust Him to know what He's doing. I've discovered that God places ideas in our minds for a reason: He has a plan for each of us, and He provides the time, resources, and people to help us reach our heartfelt goals. If you are obedient to God's Word and are committed to fulfilling His plans for your life, you can face the fear of decision making with the assurance that God is in control of the situation.

These past years as a full-time professional speaker have not been without trial and error, loss and aggravation, heartache and tears. But the good times far outweigh the bad times. God knew what He was doing.

Prayer

Lord, I'm glad You know everything. You know what I should be doing and when I should do it. You know my purpose in life and how my experiences build wisdom and faith for future challenges. When I become fearful of the future, remind me that You are sufficient in everything. You are in control. It's great to realize that I'm not out here making decisions alone. The Holy Spirit is guiding me all the time. May that blessed assurance make me act boldly, even when I feel afraid. Amen.

God's Word to You

I am the LORD, your God, who takes hold of your right hand and says to you, Do not fear; I will help you (Isaiah 41:13).

Affirmation

Even when I am afraid, I can confidently follow the path God has laid out for me.

13

Did You Say My Book?

The telephone rang at my office around ten o'clock. An executive from the National Speakers Association (NSA) asked me to have my book at the NSA Dallas Convention site within a month. I was scheduled to be the keynote speaker for a general session of the NSA, and all keynote speakers were expected to be published.

"My book?" I sputtered. "Did you say my book?"

I wasn't aware of that requirement when I accepted the pioneering opportunity to be the first black woman to speak for the NSA general session.

"A book? My book? I'm supposed to have a book?" How would I ever get a book written and published within a month? No way!

My business consultant (and daughter) Vikki was listening to me stutter and sputter, and she asked that I give the telephone to her. After discussing "the book" as if it existed, she declared, "Oh, yes, Thelma's book will be delivered by that date. You can depend on that."

What in the world had she done? She'd just put *my* reputation on the line by implying that I had a book, and she was crazy enough to tell the NSA executive it would be there within 30 days! I felt sick to my stomach; I wanted to throw up. After listening to my objections, Vikki reminded me that the speaking invitation was an honor. Was I going to blow it for lack of a book? According to Vikki, not on my life!

"How in the name of all that's right can I get a book written, published, and delivered by the deadline?" I asked. I saw no possible way of accomplishing what Vikki had just promised.

Well, quick-thinking Miss Vikki had it all figured out. "Listen," she instructed me, "you've got the outline of your seminar. You know what you're talking about. You've got the stories to go with it. While you're traveling, you can also write. Fax what you've written back to me. I'll take care of it. Leave the rest to me. Okay? Do you understand? Do it!"

Like a good businesswoman, I did it—albeit nervously. While I was writing and faxing, Vikki was doing publishing research, collecting a network of proofreaders, getting endorsements, hiring an illustrator, and lining up a book printer. My self-published 30-day book would be a masterpiece or bust!

Fortunately, we remembered to stop and pray. We asked God to give us the wisdom, knowledge, people, printer, stamina, creativity, and everything we needed to make the impossible project possible. We realized that without Him orchestrating the details, we were like a ship without a sail. We couldn't be smart enough, innovative enough, or clever enough to do this without the aid of the Holy Spirit.

Need I say that everything worked together perfectly? The book was called *Capture Your Audience Through Storytelling,* and Vikki believed it would be a bestseller. On the thirtieth day following the startling telephone call, she drove to Austin to pick up the "impossible" book that had been finished, and she delivered 1800 copies to the convention site. The day I spoke, I sold almost all the copies! Since that time, the book has been purchased by thousands of people and organizations.[1]

Perhaps you're facing impossibilities in your life—things you know you can't do on your own. You don't know how to do it or how to go about doing it. (Vikki and I didn't know how.) You don't know who to ask for help. (We didn't know who to ask.) You don't know where to go. (We didn't know where to go.) But God did! If you have projects and ideas that have lingered dormant in your mind because you've assumed that finishing or pursuing them is beyond your grasp, think again. Don't underestimate God's ability to bring "impossible" things to pass. When He places an idea in your head, trust that He has provided all it will take to bring it to fruition.

Often our biggest problem is not lack of skill or resourcefulness or time. No, it's lack of faith. We don't believe things can or will happen. God specializes in things that seem impossible! Depend on Him to guide and direct you. He wants to. Trust Him!

Prayer

Father, I really need to trust You when I have ideas or demands that seem impossible to fulfill. I see You working things out all the time, and yet I resist asking You to make the impossible possible. Your power and patience amaze me. Thank You for showing me that all I have to do is call on You for assistance, and You will gladly give it. Nothing is impossible with You. Amen.

God's Word to You

Nothing is impossible with God (Luke 1:37).

Affirmation

I bring all my challenges to God, who specializes in accomplishing things that seem impossible.

14

God Sent Us to College

When I was a girl, my family was poor and had no means of putting money aside for my college education. Granny, Daddy Lawrence, and Uncle Jim made sure I had the necessities and some of the luxuries of life, so I didn't realize we were poor or just how poor we were until I got old enough to read about poverty.

Oh, how I wanted to go to college! After the secretarial school I tried to enroll in threw me out because of the color of my skin, Granny and I became more and more determined to find a way for me to go to college. Granny talked to her employer, Mrs. Mary Less, who was a wealthy white woman living in University Park in Dallas. Granny was one of her maids. Mrs. Less asked me to come to her house to discuss my college aspirations. When I did, she offered to send me to North Texas State University. She would pay my tuition and buy my books on the condition that I kept my grades above a C average. If I got married before graduation, my husband and I would have to cover the bills.

Was I excited or what! And Mrs. Less kept her end of the bargain. Daddy Lawrence gave me five dollars a month for the Laundromat, and Granny sent me "care packages" regularly. My roommates and I cooked at our off-campus home. We walked to school so there was no need of transportation money. God made a way!

When my husband and I got married on April 1, 1961, Mrs. Less' obligation became null and void. George and I had discussed my desire to get a degree, so we continued to make that a priority. I did it! I'd gotten married, changed my major from business administration to secondary education, had a child, conceived my second one, and still graduated in 1963.

Much later, my daughter Vikki wanted to attend the University of Texas at Austin. When she applied, our family's income was high, but so was our debt load. I went to Austin during student orientation and waited for almost a week to meet with the financial counselor assigned to Vikki. Once I had a chance to talk with her, she told me that Vikki's loan of $269 had been approved. *Only that much for four years of college?* I thought. *I don't think so!* I showed her our income statement and all the bills we owed. I had to prove to her that even though we made enough money, we were living from one paycheck to the next. (That's nothing to be proud of, but back then George and I didn't have the money management skills we have now.)

The counselor tried to prove to me via the computer that Vikki's financial aid application had already been processed and there was nothing else that could be done, but after she'd spent some time attempting to pull up Vikki's records, she gave up. I finally had her attention. She consented to reenter our financial statistics, and when she ran the new data through the computer, she was able to match Vikki up with more academic scholarships and work-study funds than she needed. God knew what He had in store for Vikki's future, and He saw to it that she got her education regardless of the financial limitations of her parents.

My younger daughter, Lesa, never wanted to go to a four-year college. Her goal was to become a hairstylist and own her own business. To be a successful businessperson, she decided she needed to take business courses at Mountain View Community College in Dallas. By the time Lesa was ready to start college, we were financially prepared to send her. However, we didn't have to pay for Lesa's education either. She received a scholarship to Mountain View, and Mrs. Ella Mae Rollins paid for her beauty school education. Now Lesa is the owner of her own beauty salon where six operators help people look beautiful every week. Praise God!

Little George had the good fortune of working in a jewelry store when he was in high school. The master jeweler in that store took George under his wing and taught him all he knew about jewelry repair and design. George also attended the Gemological Institute of America to hone his skills. He now works for one of the largest jewelry companies in America.

Do you have some dreams and goals that seem unreachable? Sometimes we can't see how we can possibly accomplish our objectives. But I'm here to tell you that if you keep the faith and trust in the Lord, He will open doors that you have no idea exist. What Granny said is true: Whatever you want bad enough that's within the perfect will of God, the Lord will make a way for it to come to pass. Believe it!

Prayer

Lord God, You are awesome! You are the God of computers, education, money, and all good things that come our way. Thank You for making a way when it seems there is no way. Thank You for placing people in my life who care about my future and are willing to be used by You to accomplish Your will for my life. You are truly an omnipotent God. Help me hold on to the truth that You have everything under control. You will work everything out to accomplish Your will. Amen.

God's Word to You

Not that we are competent in ourselves to claim anything for ourselves, but our competence comes from God (2 Corinthians 3:5).

Affirmation

I trust God to accomplish His plans for me.

15

The Doctors Had Given Up

My friend Ed was distraught. She was riddled with oppression, guilt, shame, depression, anguish, and self-destroying thoughts. Overcome by these plagues, she shot herself in the head to end it all.

I got the call when I was in Austin, and I couldn't believe my ears. "Ed did what? She tried to kill herself? She has two beautiful daughters and a good husband. She's well-educated, beautiful to look at, and a Christian person. How could she do something like that?" (My understanding of depression and my friend's emotional state was obviously limited back then.)

During Sunday school classes, I'd noticed that Ed often posed questions about how God can forgive heinous sins yet not relieve us from remembering them. Occasionally she was moody and distant and behaved in ways I didn't understand. Once I asked her if anything was wrong, and she mentioned a few somewhat trivial problems—everyday struggles we all have. I took her at her word and didn't ask God for discernment or try harder to get to the heart of what was going on. Later, Ed's other friends and I talked about not seeing the signs of her depression and the depth of her despair... and how bad we felt about that.

I returned to Dallas and went to Parkland Hospital's Intensive Care Unit to see Ed. She wasn't expected to live, and the medical team had given up. I looked at Ed's swollen, dark, mutilated head and face. I was told that part of her brain had to be removed to reduce the swelling and inflammation. The prognosis was either death or life in a vegetative state.

But I believed God had a plan to do more than just keep Ed breathing. My friend Debra Young had spoken to me by phone before I got to Parkland and advised me to speak only of life and read life-giving, healing scriptures because Debra also believed with all her heart that Ed would live. "Do not believe the report by the doctors!" Debra urged. "Together, let's trust God for a miracle."

One of the members of the medical team was also a friend of mine. He pulled me aside and begged me to stop people from praying for Ed's recovery. Our praying was giving false hope to her family, he said. It was disturbing and a waste of time. My reply? "If God can make a brain, He can restore a brain." We would keep praying and reading healing scriptures.

I confess that my faith got weak during the first several weeks. I started to doubt that Ed would recover. I thought, *Well, maybe it's not God's will to heal her.* Satan was trying to influence my mind even though he knew I served a healing Jesus.

Soon Ed started moving one of her legs and responding to questions by squeezing our hands. Within a few weeks the swelling was gone. Her eyes were following us as we moved. She began to smile. Ed said she was glad she'd failed in her suicide. Through the many weeks of recovery she came to realize she had much to live for.

Eventually I asked her why she'd done it.

"At the time, I thought that was the only way out of my misery," she said. "Now I know that if I just would have talked to someone about all the guilt and anger I was carrying around inside me from childhood, I wouldn't have felt so hopeless. I'm sorry I put everybody through this. I didn't know there were so many people who cared about me."

Progressively she gained strength. Her vital signs became normal. She was sitting up and receiving visitors. Soon we were taking her riding in her wheelchair. She was moved to a rehabilitation center. After a few months she went home to her family, and within one year she went back to her job. She was not the same as she was before the shooting because she still had some motor slowness and couldn't drive her car. But members of the medical team at Parkland Hospital are now convinced (whether they admit it or not) that nothing less than a miracle of God restored her to physical health.

Ed is now in a support group where she gets ongoing counseling, and most of her immediate family members are in counseling as well. Each time I see Ed, I see a different person. More and more she is becoming whole. She smiles often and is happy, content, and growing.

At one of my seminars a year after the incident, Ed told her story to the audience. She wanted people to know there are many options for solving their problems...but suicide is *not* one of them. She was glad she'd finally faced her problems and was getting professional help to handle them. Most of all, she was glad that God had forgiven her and that her family was healing from what she'd done.

God has promised that He will heal our sicknesses:

> Is any one of you sick? He should call the elders of the church to pray over him and anoint him with oil in the name of the Lord. And the prayer offered in faith will make the sick person well; the Lord will raise him up. If he has sinned, he will be forgiven. Therefore confess your sins to each other and pray for each other so that you may be healed. The prayer of a righteous man is powerful and effective (James 5:14-16).

The problem with believing that God wants to heal people lies in the fact that not everybody is healed. The apostle Paul had a thorn (pain, suffering, a physical infirmity perhaps) in his flesh. He pleaded with God three times to remove it. God refused. But He gave Paul sufficient grace and power to live with his infirmity (2 Corinthians 12:7-9).

God doesn't always act in ways we expect. Because He is sovereign, He has many options. I've seen Him heal instantly, heal through medical procedures and processes, and heal through death (the ultimate, most revered healing for a Christian, in my opinion). Just because we doubt, just because we haven't experienced healing, or just because we think miracles are not for this modern day, that doesn't stop God from doing what He promises in whatever way He chooses. The Full Life Study Bible lists ten things that can hinder healing:

- unconfessed sin
- demonic oppression or bondage
- acute anxiety
- past disappointments that undermine present faith
- people
- unbiblical teaching

- failure of the elders to pray the prayer of faith
- failure of the church to seek and obtain the gifts of miracles and healing as God intended
- unbelief
- self-centered behavior[1]

Sometimes the reason for the persistence of physical affliction in godly people is not readily apparent. In still other instances, God chooses to take His beloved saints to heaven during an illness. Until God makes His perfect will known, we can take some steps for praying and seeking His healing for our bodies:

- Be sure we are in a right relationship with God and others.
- Seek the presence of Jesus in our lives.
- Saturate our lives with God's Word.
- Examine our lives to see what changes God may desire to work in us.
- Call for the prayers of the elders of the church with the anointing of oil as well as the prayers of family members and friends.
- Attend a service where a person with a respected healing ministry is present.
- Expect a miracle—trust in Christ's power.
- Rejoice if healing comes immediately; rejoice if it does not.
- Know that God's delays in answering prayers are not necessarily denials of those requests. Sometimes God has a larger purpose in mind that, when realized, results in His greater glory and is better for us.
- Realize that if we are committed Christians, God will never forget or forsake us. He loves us too much to leave us.

I can say with all confidence that we serve a healing and delivering Jesus. My friend Ed is a living testimony. But when the God who made us and knows all about us chooses not to heal us, I believe He always gives us the strength to handle our reality, just as He did for Paul. The fact that some Christians experience healing and others do not doesn't mean God loves some people more than others. I believe He knows whom to trust with certain circumstances. He knew that Paul would be a shining example of how God can sustain His children in the midst of sickness and suffering.

Perhaps you've been pleading for healing for yourself or someone else and you're not seeing any results. Don't become frustrated and disappointed with God. Ask Him to put peace in your spirit and contentment in your soul as you persevere. Continue to pray and ask others to pray with you. Above all, praise God for the strength to make it through the situation. Maybe God is trying to tell you that He trusts you too. You can be a model for other people going through similar things.

If you see other people get healed, don't begrudge them their blessing. Be glad for them! God has a different plan for each of us, and He loves us all perfectly.

Prayer

Dear Lord, You're here when I'm sick. You're here when I'm well. You hear me when I pray. You forgive when I doubt. Sometimes my intellect gets in the way of constant faith. I wonder if You will heal someone. Yet even in my fog, You assure me You are still in complete control. Please give me the grace to persevere in faith, no matter what my circumstances. Amen.

God's Word to You

Surely he took up our infirmities and carried our sorrows... The punishment that brought us peace was upon him, and by his wounds we are healed (Isaiah 53:4-5).

Affirmation

I serve a healing Lord.

16

He'll Die at 59

I had never heard of tarot cards until one of my secretaries in years past brought them to my office. She introduced them as a fun way to look into the future or to entertain at a party. I thought, *I like to have fun. I'm curious. So why not?* I felt a little uneasy, but I didn't want to be a party pooper. Just like everybody else, I wanted to know the future. So I let her conduct several readings for me. They always yielded positive predictions. She told me about career promotions, financial success, traveling abroad, and business ventures I would have. That was good. I liked being reassured of success.

But one day she looked alarmed as she read the cards. "I hate to tell you this…" She hesitated. "You will marry twice. Your current husband will die at age 59."

"Stop!" I shouted. "I don't want to hear any more." I suddenly became sad, frightened, and suspicious of "the game." *How can cards predict when someone will die?* I thought. *Only God knows that.* Still, I was scared. My husband, George, was 46, and we'd already been married 19 years. You know the song "Wind Beneath My Wings"? Well, George is my wind. He encourages me, directs me, trusts me, loves me, supports me, listens to me, confirms me, and helps me attain peace in the midst of life's challenges. I can't imagine life without him—and I don't want to.

I begged God, "Please spare George's life!" When George turned 59, I pleaded, "Please forgive me for my foolishness, Lord. Please let my husband live." I was scared and ashamed…but I didn't share my thoughts with anyone.

As I turned to God for direction, His Word reassured me that the Holy Spirit would guide me into all truth. I don't need any tarot cards to tell me what's in store for the future. The apostle Peter taught that God gives His people messages He wants communicated; human beings can't prophesy truthfully on their own or with divination tools:

> Prophecy never had its origin in the will of man, but men spoke from God as they were carried along by the Holy Spirit. But there were also false prophets among the people, just as there will be false teachers among you. They will secretly introduce destructive heresies, even denying the sovereign Lord who bought them— bringing swift destruction on themselves. Many will follow their shameful ways and will bring the way of truth into disrepute. In their greed these teachers will exploit you with stories they have made up (2 Peter 1:21–2:3).

I came to believe that my secretary was a false prophet, and I knew God had forgiven me for my foolishness in listening to her "prophecies." I began to feel a peace about George. He's in his seventies now, healthy and quite cute! God is so merciful. Even when we stray from His teachings and experiment with demonic devices, His blood covers us. I could have become immersed in a psychic, mystical, magical culture. Satan makes it so appealing, especially when we're uncertain about our futures. But the Bible calls fortune-telling and tarot cards abominations to God (Deuteronomy 18:10-12). He does not want our reliance to be on anything but Him.

When you have a need to know your future, turn to God. Ask Him for wisdom and guidance. He knows what is in store for you, and He will reassure you that He is in control of your destiny. He promises to direct your path when you trust in Him, and He will.

Prayer

Jesus, keep me from relying on the words of others for guidance. Yes, there are Christian friends who will give me godly advice, but my total reliance must be on You. Thank You for forgiving me when I foolishly pursue the world's ways of gaining knowledge. You are the God of all truth, so I will trust in You with all my heart. Amen.

God's Word to You

When he, the Spirit of truth, comes, he will guide you into all truth. He will not speak on his own; he will speak only what he hears, and he will tell you what is yet to come (John 16:13).

Affirmation

God holds my future in His hands, and He will direct me by His Spirit within me.

17

My Child Would Never Do That!

One of the most devastating truths for parents, especially Christian parents, is that their children can and do stray from their teachings. Many kids get involved in drugs, sex, pornography, witchcraft, and gangs. Some drop out of school, abuse their parents, defy authority, and behave in other heartbreaking ways.

I remember, during the early days of my teaching career, going to a friend's house to inform her that her son was breaking into the vending machines at school. She was furious with me. "My child would never do that!" she told me emphatically. "We give him everything he needs. You'd better stop lying about him." I took her cue and stopped telling her anything about her child, but I continued to watch the situation. While his mother remained in denial, the child got more and more into a life of crime. To this day he's in trouble with the law.

There came a time in my life when shocking information was presented to me concerning children I had tried to influence. I discovered they were experimenting with drugs. At first I blamed their peers. Then I pointed the finger back at the parents and eventually at God. After all, didn't His Word say, "Train a child in the way he should go, and when he is old he will not turn from it" (Proverbs 22:6).

But that's a principle many Christians refer to without fully understanding its meaning. As I pondered the meaning of this scripture, I wondered if I were missing something. I studied the word "train" and discovered that it means "to dedicate." Parents must commit themselves to training their children in the ways of God. We must promote in our children a desire and appetite to experience God for themselves. We must dedicate our children to God and dedicate ourselves to the stewardship of the children God has entrusted us with. But we must also remember that the world, with its evil charm and cunning influence, is used to persuading children to sin. Bad choices are offered, and wrong choices are often made. Paul wrote, "All have sinned and fall short of the glory of God" (Romans 3:23).

So what's the deal? I went back and read the proverb carefully. I realized it didn't promise that our children would never stray from the path we set them on. No, it says, "When he is old he will not turn from it." As the years have gone by, I've seen that principle fulfilled. For a long time, Satan confused those children's minds and bodies, but not their souls. Even while they strayed, they never forgot their parents' biblical teachings. Scripture still rang in their ears. Respect for Jesus remained deeply embedded in their hearts. I watched a long progression of some from hostile, headstrong, immature kids to determined, funny, happy, God-loving adults. God's Word was—and is!—true. And when we feed it to our children, it will not return to Him void. Isaiah 55:10-11 declares,

> As the rain and the snow come down from heaven, and do not return to it without watering the earth and making it bud and flourish, so that it yields seed for the sower and bread for the eater, so is my word that goes out from my mouth: It will not return to me empty, but will accomplish what I desire and achieve the purpose for which I sent it.

Our God has promised never to leave us or forsake us (Deuteronomy 31:8). Children do stray, but God doesn't abandon them. We can hold fast to His promise to remain faithful to them.

Prayer

Father, sometimes I get frustrated and frightened when You let children continue their ways into bad situations and sins. I need Your strength to continue praying that they will not permanently depart from the teaching that has been instilled in them. Thank

You for the encouragement that You will never leave them or forsake them. Help me as a parent train my children in Your ways, and then give me the faith to trust You to bring the work You've begun in them to completion. Amen.

God's Word to You

The LORD himself goes before you and will be with you; he will never leave you nor forsake you. Do not be afraid; do not be discouraged (Deuteronomy 31:8).

Affirmation

I rejoice in God's faithfulness to my children and trust what He is doing in their lives.

18

Why Do You Complain?

Elle was one of the most reliable, conscientious, hardworking people in my bookkeeping department at the bank. She was always on time, worked diligently, and took little or no sick leave. She was a loyal employee. There was only one big thing wrong: She whined, complained, and behaved like a victim all the time. There was not a day that she didn't come to my office to tell me what some other employee was or wasn't doing. She seemed to feel she was the only person working and carrying the load in the department. Everyone else was talking on the telephone, going to the restroom too much, chatting with other employees, coming back late from lunch, or doing something she considered worth reporting. I wondered how she could do all the work she was doing and keep such close tabs on everybody else. She made such a habit of coming into my office to complain that every time I saw her coming, my nose started to itch. I wasn't comfortable with this state of affairs!

When I became a supervisor, I had no supervisory training, so I didn't have an educated clue about what I was supposed to do with an employee like Elle. Instead, I had to rely on common sense. One weekend, after being perplexed all week about what I needed to do to stop her complaining, I came up with a brilliant idea. I created a form that listed every employee's name, and I left space for Elle to enter information about what the other people in the department were doing. I would make her the monitor of the bookkeeping department. Job description: snoop on everybody and write it down. Report back to me with documentation of everyone's behavior.

Monday came and I asked Elle to come into my office. I asked her to be seated and told her how happy I was that she'd taken it upon herself to look out for the department's well-being. I showed her the form with all her colleagues' names and the columns to record the various behaviors that she was to monitor. I told her, "Elle, I'm making you the official watcher of the department. These people are not pulling their loads, and we need to take action. I want you to document what they're doing. If they go to the restroom and stay too long, write it down. If you think they're on a personal phone call, write it down. If you see them clocking in on more than one time card, write it down. If they go to lunch early or return late, write that down. If they talk ugly to the customers, write that down. I want you to record every wrong thing they do and report back to me in one month. When you bring the documentation to me, bring the people with you too. We'll stop this waste of company time."

Elle was horrified. She responded with an emphatic no. She didn't want to cause problems; she just thought I would want to know what was going on in the department. She couldn't bring "those people" into my office. She wasn't that brave!

Her refusal didn't surprise me. She didn't want to confront her colleagues face-to-face. She wanted to come in and just complain about them. I told Elle that if she couldn't comply with following through on what I asked, she shouldn't come in and complain.

I nipped her actions in the bud, all right. Elle never whined to me again. But the situation still perplexed me. I wondered why she thought it was so important to tattle on people. I knew she was much older than some of her colleagues and that she'd been on the job for many years. She had no academic qualifications—just the skills she'd developed on the job. She was also her sole support. Her husband was no longer around, and she lived a lonely life with only her cat to keep her company. Her son and daughter visited sometimes, but she didn't seem to have much of a social life. I was concerned about her.

Later I was promoted to supervisor of the personal banking division of the bank. Having worked first as a new accounts clerk and then as a bookkeeping supervisor, I had learned a lot about the needs of both areas. One of the most poorly managed areas in the bank was the signature cards and other account documents. Those documents were used by several departments, but no one was in charge of holding people accountable for taking them out of the files and returning them. More often than not, someone would come to look for a file, and nobody would know where it was. The situation needed attention…and I had the perfect solution!

I made Elle the official guardian of the signature cards and resolution files. She was free to rearrange the files in a more functional way so she could get to them easily. She developed a form like a library rental card to check the documents in and out. On the form were the name and department of the person, the time of day, the due date, and any other information Elle thought pertinent.

I've never seen anyone perk up and look as needed and important as Elle did. What she'd really wanted all along was to be assured that her job was secure. I discovered that her whining and complaining were smokescreens for what was really happening inside. Elle was scared of being replaced by someone who was younger or had more education. By creating that job for Elle, I gave her what she needed. She was able to regain her confidence and be proud of the job she was doing without the interference of "those other people." When it was time for Elle to retire, she did so with dignity, secure that she'd done a good job.

Sometimes people we think are chronic whiners, complainers, or victims may be sending us a message. They may be trying to tell us that they're afraid and need assurance and support. My experience with Elle helped me be less critical of people who exhibit similar behavior. I've learned there are reasons why people act the way they do.

Just as Elle was acting out of fear, so do many Christians. Behavioral experts believe most people have four basic fears:

- fear of failure
- fear of rejection
- fear of risk or loss
- fear of success

And I'm sure everybody has experienced all these at one time or another. That's human. However, the Bible has something to say about how Christians should respond to fear: "Fear of man will prove to be a snare, but whoever trusts in the LORD is kept safe" (Proverbs 29:25). Fear can be a reliable deterrent to unsafe and harmful situations or it can paralyze our efforts to move from one place to another in our lives.

When I'm afraid, if I acknowledge the fear and allow myself to analyze why I'm afraid, I usually discover I don't know how to do something or am unsure how it will turn out if I do it. The Bible is full of passages that console me and give me strength as I walk through that period of fear. I also usually talk about it with another Christian I know who will offer me godly counsel. Then I either tackle the situation with all the ammunition possible or I delegate the tasks to someone with more expertise. I try to remember that when I'm obedient to God and work to satisfy His will, I can claim Isaiah 54:4: "Do not be afraid; you will not suffer shame. Do not fear disgrace; you will not be humiliated."

When Elle was afraid for her job, I didn't shame her. Through concern and observation, and using common sense, I eliminated the undesirable behavior...and eventually, after understanding more about her situation and being in a better position myself, I could do something to help ease her fear.

Whatever your fear, God has someone or something in place to help you. Whining, complaining, and behaving like a victim are not viable ways to resolve anything. Such behavior only makes the situation worse because each time you act on your fear without resolving the main issue, you're creating a stronger habit instead of dispelling it. Problems become more intense and ingrained.

You can change your behavior! These steps will help:

- Think about the things that cause you the most fear.

- Ask yourself why you're so afraid.

- Talk about the fear with someone you trust.

- Ask God to help you overcome it.

- Study what the Bible says about fear.

- Sing praises to God or listen to music that gives praise to God.

- Choose to release the fear.

- Watch God replace your fear with confidence!

Prayer

Father, I'm so glad I can call You Father. Good fathers listen to their children's fears and do something to help them overcome them, and I know You're the best Father of all! There are so many places in the Bible where You tell me not to fear because You are my refuge, my help, my strength. You take pleasure in protecting me. How grateful I am that when I am afraid, You never shame me. You deliver me and set my feet upon the firm foundation of Jesus. Amen.

God's Word to You

God did not give us a spirit of timidity, but a spirit of power, of love and of self-discipline (2 Timothy 1:7).

Affirmation

I never have to fear because God is taking loving care of me.

19

Who Likes Criticism?

I don't know of anyone who really enjoys being criticized. But whether we like it or not, criticism is what all of us get at one time or another. Sometimes constructive criticism is easier to take than ruthless faultfinding, but criticism is criticism. It's rarely pleasant.

One day I was preparing to go into a seminar when a woman I didn't know walked up to me and said bluntly, "Your hair sure is an ugly color." (Admittedly, I kept cosmetic companies in business because at that time I colored my hair every six weeks. That particular week my hair was "Sparkling Sherry.")

I responded to this lovely woman, "Thank you. I'm glad you were paying attention to my hair. I color it every six weeks. The next time I do it, I'll remember what you said. It's always great to have an unbiased opinion."

She was speechless. I had taken her power away. Perhaps she thought she could make me feel bad, but she was wrong. The fact is, I had looked in the mirror that morning and left home pleased with the way I looked. I had a choice when she'd said those critical words to me. I could respond with hostility and anger. I could ignore her. I could use my sense of humor. I chose the latter. I turned a potentially negative statement into a positive response.

Some of the best growing I've ever done has been the result of criticism, whether constructive or destructive. In my opinion, constructive criticism occurs when someone addresses the situation instead of the person. For example: "Betty, I have some questions about this report because it doesn't seem to be complete. Can you tell me what to look for or how it can be corrected?" Destructive criticism tears down the person instead of addressing the situation appropriately: "Betty, you made a mistake on this report. Can't you ever complete a task right? Correct this and bring it back."

One of the most powerful people in my early corporate career was an officer at a bank where I worked. She could correct me and criticize me, yet make me happy. When I goofed on an account, she would come quietly to my desk and ask to speak to me in private. Her comments generally ran along these lines: "Thelma, you're learning this business quickly. I'm proud of your progress. We do have a situation that needs your attention, though. 'Mrs. Whoever' called and said her checks were ordered incorrectly. I see that your name is on the order. Will you please find out what happened, who was affected by what happened, and note how we can prevent this from happening again? Please get back to me before leaving today if possible. Thank you. I know you'll take care of it for us."

Did I ever feel important! I thought, *She trusts me to get this information to her.* Boy, I'm good. As I went through the process of getting the information, I learned more about how each department depended on the others, how to be more observant, and so forth. The bank officer was gently making sure I discovered how to do the task correctly.

Even though we don't enjoy being criticized, we must admit we learn some things about ourselves that we'd have never known had we not been criticized. Over the years, I've learned techniques for taking the sting out of receiving criticism so I can benefit more readily from it. These tips help me, and they might help you too.

- I consider the source. Is the person criticizing me genuinely interested in my well-being?

- I consider the circumstances. Am I clear on the circumstances that caused the criticism?

- If the criticism is appropriate and accurate, I'll agree with it. Who is going to argue with me when I'm agreeing with her?

- If I wish to have more explanation concerning the situation, I ask for it. Getting complete information about why someone said something or what's wrong with something is another way to learn.

- If I don't agree but don't want to have a damaged relationship, I
evade the issue by using noncommittal words such as "maybe,"
"I guess," "it seems," "possibly," "perhaps," "I'll try," "you think?"
and other phrases that don't cost me anything but let the person
know I'm hearing her.

Maybe one reason I've been married as long as I have is that I use that last technique with my husband! Sometimes when he's fussing at me about something, I say, "Honey, perhaps you're right. Maybe I need to listen to you more. The next time this happens, I'll try to pay more attention. Thank you for calling this to my attention." I'm not admitting to anything, but what I say sure makes him feel good.

On the other hand, criticism can be very wise counsel when accepted with an open mind. The book of Proverbs talks a lot about this. For instance, Proverbs 12:15 says, "The way of a fool seems right to him, but a wise man listens to advice." And Proverbs 15:22 says, "Plans fail for lack of counsel, but with many advisers they succeed." Remember, when you're faced with criticism, you have a choice. You can get hostile and defensive or you can respond positively. A wise person takes criticism and extracts from it what can help him grow. A foolish person denounces criticism and stunts his growth.

So be wise, and choose to grow from criticism.

Prayer

Lord, You use some of the most unique methods to help me become what You want me to be. Criticism doesn't make me feel good, but wise counsel is so important to You that the wisest man who ever lived, King Solomon, took a lot of time to write the book of Proverbs under Your direction. Frankly, God, I can always use feedback to help me become a more excellent servant for You. Help me to take it in the right spirit and use it wisely. Amen.

God's Word to You

Listen to advice and accept instruction, and in the end you will be wise (Proverbs 19:20).

Affirmation

I will listen to criticism with an open mind and
take from it only what will help me grow.

20

A Recovering Perfectionist

We never talked about perfection when I was growing up. I think it was just a given. I remember having to get up every morning and make my bed perfectly. I had to wash and dry the dishes and stack them perfectly in the cabinets. Straightening up the linen closet and arranging the towels perfectly was another chore. I was expected to iron my dresses perfectly and bleach my clothes so the whites were perfectly white.

At school I had to have perfect attendance. My homework had to be flawless—within the lines and complete. My lunch pail was packed carefully so that none of the foods would touch the others and spoil the taste. The pail was aired out each afternoon so it would be perfectly fresh for the next day.

At church I was expected to be a nice, quiet, intelligent girl. I learned my Bible verses and hymns and recited and sang perfectly. The one time I forgot my lines was the worst day of my life up to that point.

Uncle Jim and Aunt Allene took me to fine restaurants in our neighborhood and taught me table manners and etiquette so I'd have perfect social graces. I designed and directed all the elements of my wedding, including staying up all night before the big day to make sure it would be perfect. When I look at my wedding pictures now, I marvel at the beauty of the sanctuary and the standing-room-only crowd that attended. But I wonder why somebody didn't notice that my hoop slip was longer than the length of my dress!

After marriage, I attempted to be a perfect wife and mother. I had no idea that wives and mothers had to do so much stuff. I was the one who had to make the stripes in the towels hang straight, pull the sheets taut before making the bed, and keep the kitchen spick-and-span. For years I tried to live up to my standards. In fact, I didn't know they were unreasonable until my body rebelled. I started having headaches, passing out, and being depressed to the point of being hospitalized. My doctor and a team of psychiatrists ran all kinds of tests and uncovered my problem: I was trying to be perfect. I was trying to live up to what I thought everybody's expectations were for me. I wanted to please everyone perfectly.

My doctor demanded that changes be made in my thinking patterns and activities. He even talked with George about the problem. Soon I learned for the first time that all the things I compulsively focused on were not as important to George as I thought. He never said he wanted me to do everything perfectly; I just assumed he did.

Changing ingrained behavior isn't an easy thing to do, so the doctor suggested I take baby steps. I was to resist the urge to make my bed the instant my feet hit the floor. I was to practice not cleaning off the table the minute we were finished with a meal. The first time I left the bed unmade, I felt guilty and untidy. Thirty minutes were all I could take! But that was a start. It's been nearly 30 years since I stopped trying to be perfect. It's been about 20 years since I could detect a real difference in my thinking and truly let go of my self-imposed guilt for not doing everything "right."

I've coined my own definition of perfectionism: "a neurotic, destructive syndrome designed to make people feel guilty when they don't do what they think everybody else in the world wants them to do." From personal experience I've found that true perfectionists are pains in the neck. They never live up to their standards…and neither does anyone else. When they make a mistake, it follows them around like a dark cloud, ruining their day and marring their interactions with others.

Someone gave me this writing one day, which contrasts self-limiting perfectionism with the self-liberating pursuit of excellence.

> Perfection is being right. Excellence is willing to be wrong.
> Perfection is fear. Excellence is taking a risk.
> Perfection is anger and frustration. Excellence is powerful.
> Perfection is control. Excellence is spontaneous.

> Perfection is judgment. Excellence is accepting.
> Perfection is taking. Excellence is giving.
> Perfection is doubt. Excellence is confidence.
> Perfection is pressure. Excellence is natural.
> Perfection is the destination. Excellence is the journey.
>
> AUTHOR UNKNOWN

One reason so many of us compulsively pursue perfection is that we don't understand what God expects of us. We read Jesus' words in Matthew 5:48, "Be perfect, therefore, as your heavenly Father is perfect," and we wonder if God is the ultimate taskmaster. But when the Bible uses the word "perfect" (NKJV) or "blameless" (NIV), it usually means "complete," and not "flawless."

The Bible says that "Noah was a just man, perfect in his generations. Noah walked with God" (Genesis 6:9 NKJV). *Strong's Concordance* translates "perfect" in this passage as "complete, full, undefiled, upright, full of integrity and truth." Genesis 17:1 says, "When Abram was ninety-nine years old, the LORD appeared to him and said, 'I am God Almighty; walk before me and be blameless.'" "Blameless" has the same meaning for Abram as it did for Noah. Psalm 37:37 says, "Consider the blameless, observe the upright; there is a future for the man of peace." "Blameless" in this passage means "complete, pious, gentle, and dear." So when Jesus told us in Matthew to be perfect like our Father, He meant for us to be complete, full grown, and mature.

When I consider my definition of perfection during my compulsive days, I realize I was striving to do everything well so I'd be considered competent and responsible. It is so refreshing to me now not to have to be "perfect" by the world's definition. Only Jesus Christ was a perfect human being, and because He made the perfect sacrifice for me, I am perfect (complete) in Him. I have nothing to prove.

The next time you get down on yourself because life isn't going the way you planned and you can't do something perfectly, don't beat yourself up, don't blame other people, and don't keep striving for the impossible. Perfectionism is a sickness, and Jesus is the Healer. Look to the Source of your strength for help and comfort and contentment. Rest in Him.

Prayer

Oh, God, how wonderful I feel knowing I don't have to be perfect. What a relief to know that You understand my human inadequacies and are ready, willing, and able to bear them for me. When I look to You alone for my completeness, the pressure is lightened, the stress is decreased, the tasks are made easier. Thank You for being a God of mercy, grace, and strength who loves me. Amen.

God's Word to You

[God] said to me, "My grace is sufficient for you, for my power is made perfect in weakness" (2 Corinthians 12:9).

Affirmation

When I cannot meet the world's standards,
I rest in the knowledge that God's standard
is completeness in Him.

21

Victims or Victors?

One of the hardest demands God makes of His children is the one that calls us to love our enemies—to forgive people who have knowingly and willfully violated us physically, emotionally, or spiritually. When we are hurt by the infidelity of a spouse, abuse from a loved one, vicious gossip, unfair treatment at work, crime, or humiliation, the wound goes deep. Anything that threatens our safety, security, integrity, intelligence, or character is difficult to cope with, much less to forgive.

At one time in my life, I really hated some people who had hurt me. God knew that sometimes I really wanted to see them dead. I obsessed about their deeds against me and daydreamed about what I would do to get even. Yes, I really did! Here I was, thinking I was a good Christian woman, but I had tons of hatred and vengeance, wrath and hostility in my heart. I believe my unforgiving spirit eventually manifested itself in a two-and-a-half-year bout with a physical ailment called phlebitis. Having pains and redness in my left leg and wearing heavy elastic stockings to aid blood circulation became part of my daily routine. Medicines my doctors prescribed weren't helping. Not even the painful injections I got in my stomach to aid blood coagulation were helping. I was in the hospital several times, and I missed a lot of work. Whenever I sat down, I had to elevate my legs to keep a blood clot from forming and possibly killing me. I was a mess!

Thank God for true friends. Orniece Shelby came to see me and offered a different prescription altogether. "Thelma, I really believe you'll get well if you forgive the people who have hurt you. Whatever it is, let it go!"

To that insulting statement, I made an emphatic, uncharacteristically harsh reply, telling her where she could go for saying something like that to me. (I was not as strong in my Christian walk as I am now.)

Several weeks passed, and I wasn't getting better. Orniece came to see me again and told me the same thing: "Thelma, Baby, I believe you'd get well if you would just forgive them for what they did to you." That time I wasn't quite so defensive. My friend had planted a seed of truth, and the Holy Spirit was watering it.

By the third time Orniece urged me to forgive, I'd become convinced that something might indeed be going on inside me, stifling the healing process. I decided to accept my friend's prescription, which included reading my Bible and asking God to help me forgive. Notice, I was not to ask to be healed of phlebitis but to be given a forgiving heart.

Over time I began to submit to God's will and forgive. I asked Him to make it convenient for me to see the people I hated and to help me tell them, "I forgive you." One Thursday after my regular weekly laboratory visit where the technician tested my blood for a medication adjustment, I stopped by an automobile parts store. Guess who was there? Yes, two people who were parties to my betrayal. The two people I hated. I had asked God to make it convenient for me to tell them I forgave them, and He did. (Watch what you pray for, you might get it sooner than you think.)

My heart was pumping overtime. My hands began to sweat. My tongue was heavy. I thought about the vow I'd made to God, and I remembered that it's better to never make a vow than to make one and break it (Ecclesiastes 5:5). My moment of truth had arrived. With fear and trembling, I approached my enemies, told them that I was keenly aware of the things that had happened and how hurt I had been, but I wanted them to know that I forgave them. They were shocked.

When I left their presence, I felt as if the weight of the world had been lifted off my shoulders. I was delighted by my ability to express genuine forgiveness to them after seriously wanting something bad to happen to them for so long. At that moment, I became a victor instead of a victim. God restored the joy of my salvation. I was given back my song of praise. Boy, did I feel different!

When I returned home the following Thursday from my weekly laboratory visit, my doctor called me to report how pleased he was with my progress. He said the tests showed that I had begun to respond favorably to the medication. Tremendous progress continued for the next few weeks until I decided, "No more medicine." I knew deep in my heart that I was delivered from my grudges and hatred, and I was healed of my dreaded condition. Praise the name of Jesus!

Now please don't misunderstand me. I'm not saying that all people who are sick are in that condition because they harbor resentments. But I am saying that hatred and lack of forgiveness will manifest themselves in one way or another. Trying to get even with people who have hurt us drains our energy and diminishes our productivity. Holding on to our hurts will always have negative effects on our lives.

Sometimes we just don't want to let go of our grudges and heartaches. We want to hold on to them and watch our enemies suffer. We look for opportunities to bring up the past and rub the guilty persons' faces in what they've done. But while we're in the "get back at them" stage, we are constantly rehashing their actions toward us, our reactions toward them, and our hopes for their destruction. Resentment spreads like cancer, eating away at the soul. It destroys our hopes and relationships. I know from experience.

Have you been there? Are you there now? Maybe your lack of forgiveness has caused guilt feelings, oversensitivity, physical ailments, poor relationships, problems on the job, lack of trust in others, paralyzing fear of the unknown, or something else that hinders your experience of the abundant life Christ promises. If this is true, you can ask God to help you become willing to forgive and ultimately to speak forgiveness to those who have hurt you.

Jesus told us that if we are unwilling to forgive, we will not be forgiven (Matthew 6:15). Friend, don't miss out on God's precious grace. Allow the Holy Spirit to administer the healing medicine of forgiveness.

Prayer

Father, how deeply I appreciate the fact that You forgive me for every wrong I've ever done. You love to forgive! The beautiful thing about Your forgiveness is that You never rub my nose in my past transgressions. You choose to forget my sins. Please grant me a forgiving heart like Yours. Help me let go of my grudges and

bitterness so I can be a victor instead of a victim. The power to
forgive is such sweetness in my soul. Amen.

God's Word to You

If you forgive men when they sin against you, your heavenly Father will also forgive you. But if you do not forgive men their sins, your Father will not forgive your sins (Matthew 6:14-15).

Affirmation

Because I am forgiven by God for my transgressions,
I forgive my enemies for theirs.

22

Praise Is a Two-way Street

I've always enjoyed praising God in song. Singing praise and worship songs has calmed me when I'm upset, adjusted my attitude when it got out of whack, given me patience when I'm restless, and infused me with the sheer pleasure of making music to the Lord. I love to sing!

For years, the idea of producing a music album was tucked in the far recesses of my mind. I thought about it now and then, but I assumed the probability was remote. My children and several friends had suggested I produce an album, but frankly I didn't think my voice was recording quality. I sang in church sometimes, and I was always singing at home. Sometimes I sang at the end of my speaking engagements and occasionally at weddings. That was certainly no reason to get my hopes up about being a recording artist.

One evening I was driving south on Interstate 35 in Dallas, and the thought again occurred to me to cut a music album. *Now what is this, Lord? I can't do that! Besides, I'm in the middle of preparing for my annual "Becoming a Woman of Excellence" retreat.* I told Him, *I don't have time to deal with a music album.* (Yes, sometimes I argue with God.) I put the thought out of my mind and continued with my plans for the retreat.

A month later the retreat was behind me, and the idea about recording an album jumped into my mind again as I was driving to work one morning. This time the voice within got more specific. The Holy Spirit seemed to be directing me: "Cut the album the weekend before Thanksgiving." God had my attention. *All right, all right! Whatever You say, Sir!* (I ought to know by now that I'll never win when I argue with God.) I called my daughter Vikki, and we started planning immediately.

We began putting the pieces together for what we called a Thanksgiving Gala, to be held at St. John Missionary Baptist Church. Vikki made all the arrangements with the recording company, worked out stage and set decorations and lighting, obtained music permissions and contracts, musicians and soloists. My office staff busily prepared invitations, news releases, publicity, and every other detail to make the recorded worship program a success and honoring to the Lord. My role in the entire project was minimal. I would simply sing along with other "unknowns" whom we believed had anointed voices and would allow their talents to be used for the glory of God.

The night of the Gala arrived. The audience attendance was good. The stage and lighting were warm and worshipful. The recording company was skilled and professional. The music was outstanding! People talked about the sacredness and quality of the program for a long time. The recording, *Jesus, We Give Thanks,* comforted people in hospitals and nursing homes, and blessed people in their homes, offices, and cars all across the nation. People called and faxed in orders for more and more copies. Some people ordered 20 at a time! (Although that music is no longer available, my latest CD called *His Glorious Grace: Testimony in Song* is available through my website: www.thelmawells.com.)

I cringe when I think what a major ministry opportunity I would have missed had I continued to ignore the Lord's prompting to produce an album. God had a definite plan in mind: He wanted me to help His people praise Him. He has put the desire to worship deep within our hearts, and He wants us to raise our hearts and voices to Him. The word "praise" is recorded in the Bible 216 times (according to *Strong's Concordance of the Bible*), so it must be pretty important! Psalm 22:3 says that God inhabits our praise. When we worship, He is in our midst. That's why there is such great pleasure in honoring God with our praise for all He is and does and for His great love for us.

In Zephaniah 3, the prophet painted a magnificent picture of this holy love. After God condemned the religious people of the land for their moral decay, His merciful nature shone forth. He promised to gather His true children, the ones who offered Him praise, and sustain them as He destroyed His enemies. He would restore their fortunes before their very eyes and give them back their joy. And God would respond to His people's praise with His own:

> The LORD your God is with you, he is mighty to save. He will take great delight in you, he will quiet you with his love, he will rejoice over you with singing (verse 17).

How awesome to know that Almighty God rejoices over us when we praise Him! Consider Psalm 147:1:

> Praise the LORD. How good it is to sing praises to our God, how pleasant and fitting to praise him!

It is good and pleasant to praise the Lord. Good for Him; pleasant for us! Praise is a two-way street. Hallelujah!

Prayer

Jesus, thank You for being an awesome God who deserves all my praise. You are the Holy One. You are the Precious One. You are the Alpha and Omega, the Master of everything. I love You, Lord. I hold You in highest esteem. How thrilling to hear You sing back to me when I lift my voice to You in praise! Amen.

God's Word to You

Let everything that has breath praise the LORD (Psalm 150:6).

Affirmation

When I praise the Lord, He sings back to me with joy.

23

His Eye Is on the Sparrow

My daughter Vikki was independent, adventurous, and courageous as a twenty-something young lady, and she had always wanted to see the world. She set out on an 18-country tour, and the first six months of her voyage from Dallas to Europe, and from Asia to India went well. The next stop was to be Egypt, but God intervened. She called me from an airport in India and said, "I'm not going on to Egypt as I'd planned. Something's telling me I need to leave and go to Germany. I'll call you in a few days when I get there."

Little did she know that the day after her departure, the day she was scheduled to be in Egypt, war broke out. Operation Desert Storm had begun. Had she gone to Egypt or remained in that area of the world, the possibility of her getting trapped there by the military is frightening to think about. Many Americans were stuck and weren't permitted to leave for a number of days.

My son, George Jr., lived in California for a short time. He wasn't accustomed to or familiar with gang activity; his knowledge of gangs was limited to what he'd seen on television. But he learned quickly after living in the Los Angeles area for about a week. One day he wore the wrong color shirt. George, an unsuspecting, happy-go-lucky young man, was leisurely walking to his friend Daryl's house. Daryl was watching out his window and realized the danger George was in. Daryl yelled to George to hurry and get in the house before he was seen. Praise God, George listened. Just as he ran into the house, a car full of gang members drove by the house making loud, frightening threats.

George had another "scared stiff" experience while in California. He'd finished working at Sears that day, and on his way home he noticed a man who looked safe for him to speak to. Remember, George is from Texas. We speak to people whether we know them or not. George greeted the man with his usual friendliness, expecting a nod or verbal greeting in response. George got more than he bargained for. The man pulled out a gun, used profane invectives, said he was waiting for someone to kill that day, and George was the one.

Some people happened to be coming toward them, and George had gotten enough distance between him and the gunman to start running toward the people for protection. The crazy gunman turned away from George and went in the opposite direction. Whatever the gunman's rationale was for not following through on his murderous urge, I believe God showed up again and spared George's life one more time.

In every situation, whether ordinary or life threatening, God assures us that He keeps His eye on us and even knows the number of hairs on our heads. Absolutely everything that can happen to us—good, bad, and indifferent—God knows and cares about. God is concerned about us all the time and in every area of our lives. He promises that we are *never* away from His presence.

Does that mean nothing bad will ever happen to us? No. But it does mean that we can have inner peace in this dangerous world. Jesus declared, "I have told you these things, so that in me you may have peace. In this world you will have trouble. But take heart! I have overcome the world" (John 16:33).

God has promised to watch over His children. Every trial, tribulation, question mark, perplexity, decision, burden, disappointment, heartache, calamity, tragedy, turmoil, loss, danger, exclusion, accusation, threat, and act of the devil is within the scope of God's knowledge and care. He is sovereign, and He knows the outcome of whatever befalls us. He has already worked it out. His ministering angels protect us. His precious blood covers us. His grace and mercy go before us. In Isaiah 43:2-3, He says,

> When you pass through the waters, I will be with you; and when you pass through the rivers, they will not sweep over you. When you walk through the fire, you will not be burned; the flames will

not set you ablaze. For I am the LORD, your God, the Holy One of Israel, your Savior.

With that kind of assurance, I am confident that God is with me wherever I am and in whatever my circumstances. He's watching over me…and He's watching over you!

Prayer

How consoling, Lord, to know without a doubt that everywhere I go, You are watching over me. I'm so glad You're omniscient, omnipresent, and omnipotent, that You're not limited by time, space, gravity, or atmosphere. Thank You for proving Your nearness in my scary experiences. And thank You that no matter what I encounter in this world, You have already overcome it. Amen.

God's Word to You

Are not two sparrows sold for a penny? Yet not one of them will fall to the ground apart from the will of your Father. And even the very hairs of your head are all numbered. So don't be afraid; you are worth more than many sparrows (Matthew 10:29-31).

Affirmation

No matter what circumstances I face in this world,
I have no reason to fear because God is watching over me.

24

Our God Reigns!

The daughter of one of my good friends called me recently and asked me to speak for an annual religious conference. She was Muslim. I reminded her that I am a Christian. She replied that she knew I was a Christian, but her mother and sister-in-law had told her I was an excellent speaker and her organization should ask me to speak at their conference. I explained to her that Jesus Christ is Lord of my life, and that I talk about Jesus in my speeches. She said, "Oh, just talk about male–female relationships and how you have stayed married all these years. We want a mature lady who can be a role model for us."

I hesitated before saying yes. As I thought about it, I was reminded of an occasional prayer of mine: "Lord, please give me opportunities to witness for You." And then I was reminded of what He'd told me to do once when I was lying on the floor talking to Him. I'd gotten the impression that He wanted me to accept every speaking invitation as an opportunity to proclaim Him. Jesus told His disciples, "The harvest is plentiful but the workers are few" (Matthew 9:37). Was I willing to work to gather the harvest? In my spirit, God reminded me that He would be with me. He goes before me, stays beside me, and follows after me. I accepted the invitation.

When the day arrived, there were a lot of women at the New Hope Baptist Church where the conference was held. (I thought it rather strange to hold a Muslim conference inside a Baptist church.) When the time came for me to speak, I began. "I greet you in the name of Jehovah, Yahweh, my

Creator and my God, and in the name of Yeshua, Jesus Christ, my Lord and Savior." I reasoned that if they can greet assemblies by acknowledging Allah, I could greet them in the name of the Lord. You could have heard a pin drop! But I had set the stage for who I am in Christ.

I proceeded to talk about my marriage of more than three decades and how God had brought George and me out of some of the pitfalls. I shared how I called on Jesus all the time to help me and how the Holy Spirit guided me with wisdom I couldn't possibly have gotten on my own. I told them they too could have the blessing of this kind of wisdom, and that biblical wisdom yields peace and joy. I revealed how the joy of the Lord can destroy hostility and bitterness between spouses and then spill over into the community. Frequently while I was speaking, many of the women shouted in agreement. There were spurts of applause, and by the end of my speech women were standing up, happily nodding their heads, waving their handkerchiefs, clapping their hands, and saying, "Yes! Speak on, Sister. Tell the truth!" I can't say if they fully accepted the truth that Jesus Christ is the Messiah and Savior of all humankind, but I can say they didn't reject outright what I was saying. Many of them thanked me for delivering such a powerful message.

Before I went to the conference I spent a lot of time in prayer. I asked the Lord to help me speak and act in love and peace. I didn't want to do anything that would negatively affect my Christian witness to those Muslim women. I prayed that God's ministering angels would be there to help me do my Master's will. God heard my prayers and granted abundant grace. My friend tells me that her daughter and other members of her group still talk about how encouraging and enlightening my words were. Glory to God!

I know wherever God leads me, He will give me the wisdom to represent Him rightly. I also have come to realize that all people are born with an innate desire to be in fellowship with the Creator. The world is looking for God in so many different places. Christians have been given a mandate to go into all the world and preach the gospel to all nations, and I accept that calling as my own (Matthew 28:19-20). God gives me opportunities to represent Him, not because I'm so wonderful and know so much, but because I'm willing and available for Him.

Sometimes it's scary to address people with beliefs so different from my own, but I count it a blessing and privilege to be entrusted with such strategic assignments. I delight in the words of the prophet Isaiah:

How beautiful on the mountains are the feet of those who bring good news, who proclaim peace, who bring good tidings, who proclaim salvation, who say to Zion, "Your God reigns!" (Isaiah 52:7).

Prayer

Father, the whole world is looking for a relationship with You, whether the people know it or not. Some look to various religions, cults, customs, traditions, and works. I'm so glad You provided the way to You through Your Son, Jesus Christ. Even when Your Son's name is used in places where it's not popular, people notice His presence. You reign over every place, person, principality, purpose, and possibility, and You provide a forum for the truth to be revealed. Thank You that I can say with confidence, "My God reigns!" Amen.

God's Word to You

The LORD reigns forever, your God, O Zion, for all generations. Praise the LORD (Psalm 146:10).

Affirmation

I trust God to reveal Himself throughout the universe, and I accept His call to proclaim His good news to all people.

PART 2

God Will Make a Way

Praise be to the LORD,
who has given rest to his people Israel
just as he promised.
Not one word has failed of all the good promises
he gave through his servant Moses.

1 KINGS 8:56

God Fulfills All His Promises

"The Lord will make a way somehow." Granny's faith-filled words still ring in my ears. She taught me that God is the God of the morning, noonday, afternoon, evening, and midnight hour. God is the ruler of the planets, sun, moon, stars, atoms, space, time, energy, gravity, formulas, hypotheses, birth, breath, life, and death. He controls our going out and our coming in. He blesses our sitting down and our standing up. He's written our names on His hands, and if we let Him, He intimately directs our steps. The circumstances of our lives are no secret to Him, for He knows our innermost thoughts and desires. He knows far better than we do exactly what we need, and He has promised to meet us at every turn to show us we are precious to Him. His Word is overflowing with promises of His faithfulness to us.

Biblical scholars say there are more than 37,000 promises in the Word of God—promises to comfort us, love us, prosper us, forgive us, protect us, bless us, prepare us, reward us, and on and on. Granny always seemed so sure that God would fulfill His promises, and I wanted to grow in the kind of faith she had. I began studying God's promises out of curiosity. I started wondering what I could expect from God. What had He pledged to me personally? Although I knew He had made promises to Abraham regarding his offspring, to Moses and the people of Israel, to the disciples, and to future believers, I wondered how those promises related to me today.

As I began studying, I found myself reminiscing and reflecting. When I read, "For he will command his angels concerning you to guard you in all your ways" (Psalm 91:11), I remembered the time my car slid across the highway and crashed. Amazingly, I emerged without a scratch. When I read, "God will meet all your needs according to his glorious riches in Christ Jesus" (Philippians 4:19), I recalled the time I really needed $26,000 in three weeks, and God supplied the funds. When I read, "Train a child in the way he should go, and when he is old he will not turn from it" (Proverbs 22:6), I thought about children who were addicted to drugs throughout their youth but today are living productive lives.

I got excited! I was onto something. God's promises had been fulfilled over and over again in my daily life. I could no longer view ordinary situations—life's ups and downs—as mere coincidences. Now I could see them clearly as the real-life unfolding of God's promises. My God was a God of His word, and my life was packed with evidence of His faithfulness.

When I was a child, He rescued me and saved me. When I was a teenager, He renewed Himself in me and gave me peace and comfort. When I became a young adult, He delivered me from self-destruction. Since I've become a mature adult, He's healed my body, delivered my children, and opened doors I needed to walk through while closing doors that were not in His plans for me. God, through His Son, Jesus, has put a song in my heart and praise on my lips. He has taken the broken pieces of my life and restored them more perfectly than they were. And He wants to do the same for you. He longs to show His faithfulness to His creation.

When you walk with Him, He will reveal to you who you are in Him and what He has for you to do. He has given you His Word so you will know His thoughts toward you and His plans for you. When you hide His Word in your heart, you will have joy unspeakable as you discover that He stays true to His Word to you always.

What a mighty, tender, and awesome God we serve! That's why angels bow before Him and heaven and earth adore Him. And so do I, because He has shown me His faithfulness. My experiences confirm to me God's commitment to fulfill His Word in my life. Every story I share is true, and each promise fulfilled is a snapshot of the character of God. If God fulfills His promises in my life, then He is doing the same in yours because He's given each of us His Word. As you read about the moments that have transformed my understanding of God, I pray you will recognize and recall similar moments from your history. We all have them if we open our eyes to see.

God's promises bring great hope. As I've embraced and personally celebrated God's promises, I've felt completely reborn. Liberated. Overjoyed. May you find this same hope and joy as you discover that your Father in heaven is indeed a God of His Word. God will make a way!

> For the LORD is good and his love endures forever; his faithfulness continues through all generations (Psalm 100:5).

Prayer

Dear Jesus, I'm so comforted knowing You never go back on Your word. What You say is "yes and amen." Thank You for letting me know I can trust You to keep all your promises. I don't always understand what You're doing or why, but You never disappoint me. You are truly the living Truth. Help me cling to Your promises when times are hard. I know in due season You will bless me because You love me. In Your name I pray. Amen.

God's Word to you

The LORD is good and his love endures forever; his faithfulness continues through all generations (Psalm 100:5).

Affirmation

*I can be calm and at peace because
God keeps all His promises.*

25

Bee Your Best!

Just about everyone who is acquainted with me knows I wear a bumblebee brooch every day. People have heard me make reference to the bumblebee in many of my speeches. This is by design. My motto, "In Christ you can be the best of what you want to BEE!" has encouraged me through the thick and thins of life.

I realize the bumblebee has no power of its own to make me be my best. Some people even think it's trite. But I'm amazed that the bee is able to do what God designed it to do in spite of its scientific limitations. You see, the body of a bumblebee is too big and its wingspan too narrow for it to be able to fly aerodynamically. Yet it flies around anyway, doing what God created it to do. The bee defies the laws of nature but adheres to the law of God!

Human beings need a lot of encouragement to be able to do the things required and desired of them. Sometimes I've gotten bogged down in the pity parties of life, and I've tried to deny that I have the ability to do what God wants me to. But I know in my heart and soul that He doesn't assign me anything I can't handle. Sometimes I have to take inventory of who I am in Him by asking:

- Who am I?

- What is my mission?

- What is my vision?

- What is my passion?

- Where do I want to be now?

- How do I know I can accomplish all these things?

Let me share some of the answers I get when I ask these questions.

Who Am I?

I am a child of God with God-given talent, skill, and ability. I know that "I can do everything through him who gives me strength" (Philippians 4:13). I understand that I have intellect and common sense, but that I'm not smart enough to outthink, out give, and outdo God.

I realize that even though I do some things well, I am not a master of all trades. Therefore, I recognize my limitations. When tasks come along that I don't do well or don't need to do myself, I delegate them, hire them out, or get rid of them.

- I am a good wife, a beloved mother, and a proud grandmother.

- I enjoy making people happy.

- I am a speaker, author, singer, and businesswoman.

- I enjoy studying the Bible, going to church socials, watching Christian television, and traveling.

- I enjoy learning and staying ahead of the game.

- I'm a risk taker and adventurer.

- I'm a true friend.

- I'm attractive and enjoy dressing attractively.

- My daughter Lesa calls me a Proverbs 31 woman.

What Is My Mission?

My mission is to travel globally, extracting diamonds out of people's dust. I believe that all people have so much good in them—talent, skill, and life experiences that can help them live an abundant life through Jesus Christ. I believe my mission is to take people messages of hope, inspiration, and encouragement to motivate them to look deep inside themselves and realize their potential in Christ, as well as extract the strengths that can help them achieve their purposes in life. All of us are as frail as dust, but when given the opportunity to achieve and excel, we become stronger with each success.

What Is My Vision?

- I see myself traveling around the world, talking to huge audiences about the restoring power of God.

- I see my books appearing in every possible location in the world.

- I see people accepting Christ as a result of hearing me speak and reading my books.

What Is My Passion?

My passion is delivering the Word of God.

Where Do I Want to Be Now?

I want to be in the perfect will of God in my business, family, church, civic, leisure, academic, relational, and all other pursuits. This is a lofty desire because sometimes I don't know God's will for my life. However, within the past ten years I've used a method that seems to work for me. Before I become involved in a business venture, speak, join a committee, go on vacation, or deal with a difficult relationship, I go to the Word of God to see what the Bible has to say about the situation. Then I pray for wisdom and guidance. I know God is a God of order, and I depend on Him to bring order into whatever I'm contemplating. If I run into a lot of problems and things don't seem to be working out, and if the outer chaos is matched by an inner unease about my involvement, then I take it as a sign that I'm outside the perfect will of God. I have found that God communicates with each of us in ways we can understand, and I know I can count on Him to direct me clearly in what He has for me to do.

How Do I Know I Can Accomplish These Things?

I know I can accomplish all these goals because God doesn't give me a passion or direction that can't be accomplished in one way or another. I may not see the finished product, but He will let me see the beginning and let me know that He has someone in place to carry it further if my role is limited.

Taking a personal inventory is an example of what you can do to find out what you want to be when you "grow up." Maybe you already know. Maybe you're already being what you want to be. But I've discovered that when people get what they want, they usually want more or something different. "To BEE my best," I must stay in contact with God and with myself. I must never get so busy that I am out of touch with God's will and my own best interests.

If you want to be your best, encourage other people. Compliment them. Do something nice for them without expecting anything in return. Pray. Read your Bible. Read good books. Go to church. Enjoy fun activities. Watch what you eat. Take a vacation. Relax. Smell the roses. Seek God! Continue doing what keeps you in close touch with Him. He knows the plans He has for you and how He will accomplish them through you.

Prayer

Wonderful Master, You give me opportunities to BEE my best. You're the perfect example of what is the best. Your guidelines for daily living set the stage for the finale of what is best in Your sight. When I take inventory of myself, You are with me, evaluating the way I live, seeing if I am obedient to Your course for my life. Your way is narrow but straight. If I stay on the path You direct, I will have few delays and no fatalities. Thank You for Your encouragement. Thank You that You created me and Your plans for me were established before I began. If I am ever out of line with Your mission, vision, and passion for me, quickly let me know. Amen.

God's Word to You

"For I know the plans I have for you," declares the LORD, "plans to prosper you and not to harm you, plans to give you hope and a future" (Jeremiah 29:11).

Affirmation

In Christ I can BEE the best!

26

Angels Watching over Me

There is an angel craze these days. People—and I am one of them—are collecting angel paraphernalia (books, pictures, ceramics, lamps, jewelry, greeting cards, and all sorts of things). But I wonder if people realize the significance of angels.

One rainy October day, a woman with whom I'd met to discuss a business plan called me when she returned to her office in another state. We talked about the torrential rain, and she told me what happened when she'd stopped for gas on her way home from the airport. At the service station the attendant discovered she had a flat tire. "God sure knows how to protect us," she commented. "Just think what could have happened if I'd gotten on the freeway and had a blowout in this rain."

I believe angels were protecting her.

That same night, as I was heading home from the television station on the rain-slicked road, my car hydroplaned and glided uncontrollably from the center lane into the extreme left-hand lane. I was on a highway that was ordinarily crowded, but at that moment there was absolutely no oncoming traffic.

I believe angels were protecting me.

Several years ago the roads were icy as I traveled to Fort Worth from Dallas on Interstate 30. Just over the Oakland Street exit, I hit an icy patch that caused my car to slide from the right-hand lane across four lanes and into the median. Crash! Bang! I was stuck in a ditch with the car wheels spinning and the hood and side bent. Amazingly, I wasn't frightened. I rocked the car back and forth between first gear and reverse and managed to get out of the ditch and back on the freeway. The car then slid toward the opposite side, and cars were coming. But I was calmly praying. I saw the oncoming cars freeze in place and time. My car, without significant help from me, placed itself in the correct lane headed in the correct direction toward Fort Worth. The peace I felt made it feel like nothing bad was happening. I felt totally safe. Something stopped the cars. Something stopped time. I'm still amazed when I picture that scene in my mind today. I knew then and I know now that ministering angels held those oncoming cars in place, straightened my car out, and pointed me in the right direction.

Maybe you haven't experienced anything that dramatic. Or maybe you've had similar experiences and just thought they were coincidences. In my opinion, there are no coincidences. When we make Jesus Christ the Lord of our lives, He orders everything that happens to us. Psalm 37:23-24 says that when the Lord approves of a person's path, He makes that person's steps firm. Even if the person stumbles, he won't fall because the Lord upholds him.

In the back pages of the Ryrie Study Bible there is a complete study on the doctrine of angels. I've spent a lot of time in this study getting to know more and more about what angels are, how many there are, what form they have, what works they do, and how God uses them on behalf of believers, the church, nations, and the world.

I've heard many stories from Christians about their experiences with angels. Ruth Cummings has a powerful story. She attended a workshop where I taught about angels. Until then she'd given very little thought about angels working in her life, but after hearing what Scripture said, she decided to test what she'd learned.

Ruth and her husband, Tony, had been trying to conceive a child for nearly ten years with no success. They had spent thousands of dollars on fertility processes to no avail. They had given up on those processes. But in her soul, Ruth believed God had a baby in His plans for them.

Riding in her car one day, Ruth started talking to God. She asked Him to dispatch His ministering angels to get her baby. One month later she conceived, and today Ruth and Tony have a handsome son. Ruth knows God allowed His angels to work in their lives.

If you're unsure about the work angels do in your life, study the Word of God. Read books about angels. I believe it is imperative that we compare what any author says with the truth of the Holy Scriptures (Acts 17:11). Christians have written many good books about angels. Dr. Billy Graham's *Angels: God's Secret Agents* is one of the easiest to read and understand. Edward P. Myers' *A Study of Angels* is also good.

It's such a comfort to know that wherever we are, wherever we go, God has ministering angels available to assist us. Do you want to sing this Negro spiritual with me? Let's do it!

> All night, all day, angels watching over me, my Lord,
> All night, all day, angels watching over me.
> Now I lay me down to sleep.
> Angels watching over me, my Lord.
> Pray the Lord my soul to keep.
> Angels watching over me.
> All night, all day, angels watching over me, my Lord,
> All night, all day, angels watching over me.

Prayer

Heavenly Father, knowing Your ministering angels protect Your children gives me security as I travel through dangers seen and unseen. I appreciate how You reveal Your truths to me through circumstances and situations that I can't always explain. I know You're using those times to teach me Your truths. You have confirmed in many situations that angels work on my behalf, doing Your perfect will in my life as well as in the universe. Thank You for dispatching Your angels to protect and guide me. Amen.

God's Word to You

He will command his angels concerning you to guard you in all your ways; they will lift you up in their hands, so that you will not strike your foot against a stone. You will tread upon the lion and the cobra; you will trample the great lion and the serpent (Psalm 91:11-13).

Affirmation

*I am confident that angels work to
carry out God's will in my life.*

27

No Respecter of Persons

Early one fall morning I was walking out of the Earle Cabbell Federal Building in downtown Dallas after teaching a course for the Federal Credit Union. That particular morning I was dressed in my corporate attire and had my attaché case in hand. I was the image of a powerful corporate executive.

Walking toward me was a woman who looked tired, dirty, and unkempt. She even smelled bad. She approached me and asked, "Lady, would you give me a quarter?" I responded to her in a way I'm not proud of. Rude, arrogant, haughty, and judgmental summed up my attitude. With an alienating voice and an unfriendly look, I exclaimed to her, "I don't have a quarter!" Then I turned to walk away.

At that very moment the Holy Spirit convicted me. I turned back toward the woman and asked her why she needed a quarter. "I need to catch the bus," she replied. I told her I'd lied. I then pulled out my change purse and emptied it into her hand. She ran and caught the bus.

I crossed the street to the lot where my car was parked and slumped into the seat in tears. I was appalled. How could I have been so rude and insensitive to that woman? Sure, she was dirty, disheveled, and begging, but I didn't know her circumstances. Even if I hadn't wanted to give her a quarter, I should have been respectful of her as a human being.

I was shocked to discover that I was prejudiced—prejudiced against people because of the way they look. I'm ashamed to admit that when I first saw that woman, only three things came to mind: drugs, alcohol, "get a job." Yet I knew nothing about her. My perception caused me to be rude. I assumed something without having any facts.

As I sat in the car I thought, *That woman may have been an unemployed banker. Banks are failing in Dallas, and some of the executives I know have been without jobs for a year or more. Or she may be running away from somebody or something. I don't know her circumstances, and I certainly don't have the right to play God.*

That woman did me more good than my quarter did for her. She caused me to look more critically at my biases. Where had my bigoted thoughts come from? I don't remember having any experience that caused me to feel that way.

In this multicultural world, the list of "different" people grows constantly. People differ in ways that don't matter to some people but cause others major discomfort. I recently saw a talk show that featured a woman who learned firsthand that many people have deep prejudice against people they consider extremely fat. As an experiment, she had a "fat suit" made and wore it in many social and business situations. She was laughed at, stared at when she dined in public, and called a fat pig and other derogatory names.

I remember reading a survey that determined skin color was what caused many people to push others out of their lives within the first seven seconds of seeing them. "True Colors," the title of a 1991 documentary on *20/20*, revealed the blatant prejudice shown a young black man when he and a young white man went out to interview for jobs. Their secret mission was to test if there was real or only perceived prejudice among potential employers. The documentary confirmed an overwhelming amount of prejudice against the black man. Even though he had the same set of skills and personal attributes as the white man, he was treated completely differently during the job interviews and was never hired.

Prejudice usually comes from misinformation or distorted information about another person or group of people. In a cultural diversity class I taught once, I invited people to discuss anything about their culture they wanted others to know. In return, the other participants could ask them anything they wanted to know but had been afraid to ask. One woman didn't ask any questions. However, she was very interested in what was being said. I noticed she was almost sitting on the edge of her chair the whole time.

Shortly after the seminar, I got a heart-wrenching five-page letter from her. She said that all her life she'd been told that black men were rapists and killers. She was warned never to be alone with one. When she moved to a big city and found out she had to work where black men worked, she was petrified. She said she wouldn't go to the water fountain, restroom, or break room without someone to accompany her because so many black men were in the company. She could not understand why all the other white women weren't afraid of them. She never told anyone why she needed an escort everywhere she went. Her coworkers assumed she just liked a lot of company.

During my seminar, for the first time in her life she came to grips with the fact that she'd been sold a bill of goods about black men. She said that the healing process began that day, and she was so thankful for the startling education she received from attending my class.

As followers of Christ's teachings, Christians should have no place in their lives for prejudice against any human being. The woman who didn't look and smell as I thought she should was only one step from where I could be, were it not for the grace of God. The late Dr. Ernest Coble Estell Sr. quoted this favorite saying from his pulpit at St. John Missionary Baptist Church in Dallas: "It's one step from where I am to where you have to go." When I was a little girl, that saying didn't mean a thing to me, but now I understand it.

When Christ went to Calvary, I am so glad He had absolutely no prejudices or biases. He was no respecter of persons; He died for us all. If God were prejudiced, I might have been relegated to the you-can't-make-it-to-heaven group. I was poor and fat once, and I'll be black all my life. Praise God, none of that matters. The only things that matter are my love for God and my faith in His Son, Jesus Christ.

Prayer

Jesus, You set the pattern for my relationships with "different" people—people who don't look like me, talk like me, live like me. When You called Your disciples, You selected individuals most people would have overlooked because of their professions or social status. You chose to visit the homes of tax collectors, crooks, and outcasts. You offered Yourself to everyone by saying, "Come to me, all you who are weary and burdened, and I will give you rest." *Thank You, God! When people look down on me, exclude me, or don't respect me as a human being, I can always depend on You to love me without bias. I can also trust You to help me be better instead of bitter. Remind me to treat others the way I'd like them to treat me. Amen.*

God's Word to You

There is neither Jew nor Greek, slave nor free, male nor female, for you are all one in Christ Jesus (Galatians 3:28).

Affirmation

God loves everybody without bias, and
He enables me to do the same.

28

Oh, Blessed Savior

It was pitch-dark in the sanctuary of the St. John Missionary Baptist Church on that Easter night in 1959. I was sitting in the balcony with my teenage friends and my boyfriend, George, watching an artist tell the story of the crucifixion by drawing images with fluorescent chalk. The congregation was spellbound, captivated by the skill of the artist, the lifelikeness of the images, and the power of the message. Sound effects and hymns enhanced the presentation. People began to cry, moan, gasp, and wail at the torture of our Savior.

As the artist depicted the big drops of blood raining from the crown of thorns on Jesus' head and from His pierced body, something unexplainable happened to me. It looked to me as if those drops of blood were real. That was real blood flowing from my Savior's body! Jumping to my feet, I shouted, "He lives! He lives! I know He lives!" My shouts might have reminded the people around me of how emotional some people get when their team is winning a sporting event. I couldn't control my emotion. I remained in that state of holy ecstasy for a long time.

That was a glorious night—the night the Lord Jesus Christ confirmed to me that without a doubt He is the Savior of the world. Since then I've never doubted His reality. Sometimes my faith has gotten shaky, and I've doubted my role in making our relationship what it should be, but I've never questioned the saving grace of Jesus.

I love to sing the words of this hymn:

There is a Name I love to hear,
I love to sing its worth;
It sounds like music in my ear,
The sweetest Name on earth.

O how I love Jesus,
O how I love Jesus,
O how I love Jesus,
Because He first loved me![1]

Isaiah told of Jesus' coming hundreds of years prior to His birth:

For a child will be born to us, a son will be given to us; and the government will rest on His shoulders; and His name will be called Wonderful Counselor, Mighty God, Eternal Father, Prince of Peace…The zeal of the LORD of hosts will accomplish this (Isaiah 9:6-7 NASB).

Luke announced Jesus' birth: "Today in the town of David a Savior has been born to you; he is Christ the Lord" (Luke 2:11). Timothy told of some of Jesus' works: "It has now been revealed through the appearing of our Savior, Christ Jesus, who has destroyed death and has brought life and immortality to light through the gospel" (2 Timothy 1:10). Titus talked of His return: "while we wait for the blessed hope—the glorious appearing of our great God and Savior, Jesus Christ" (Titus 2:13). John exclaimed, "We have seen and testify that the Father has sent his Son to be the Savior of the world" (1 John 4:14). And John also declared, "For God so loved the world that he gave his one and only Son, that whoever believes in him shall not perish but have eternal life" (John 3:16).

From that Easter night in 1959 until today, I've been able to state with absolute certainty, "Jesus lives!"

If you haven't accepted Jesus, I encourage you to invite Him into your heart today. He came that you may have life and have it more abundantly. He came and died on the cross so you could live with Him forever in His kingdom. He wants to be your closest friend. Romans 10:9 tells us how to let Him into our lives: "If you confess with your mouth, 'Jesus is Lord,' and believe in your heart that God raised him from the dead, you will be saved." Confession and genuine belief are the criteria for salvation.

I've never seen Jesus in person. But on that platform at the convention that night, He became as real to me as any human being I've met. When I asked other people about the artist's rendering and how they felt that night, it seemed I was the only one who saw blood flow from the body of Jesus. That was His way of confirming Himself to me.

When you are His and He is yours, He will confirm Himself to you in your heart in a way you will always remember. It may not be at the moment you invite Him in…in fact, it could be years later. But you will know by the Holy Spirit working in your life that you are accepted into the household of faith.

Prayer

Thank You, heavenly Father, for loving me so much that You sent Your only Son to die on a cross so that I might be saved. You could have destroyed humankind with the tip of Your finger, but You didn't. Instead, You've chosen to live in each person's heart so intensely that every day we are filled by Your love. How exciting to know that one day I will see You face-to-face! That will be an indescribable day of jubilee. Amen.

God's Word to You

Salvation is found in no one else, for there is no other name under heaven given to men by which we must be saved (Acts 4:12).

Affirmation

I am saved by the blood of the Lamb of God,
who has taken away the sins of the world.

29

The Call Up Yonder

M y mama had two strikes against her all her life: She had a paralyzed right arm and foot. For the last six years of her life she was ill, and poor circulation made moving a challenge. Eventually she was confined to bed. However, her mind was alert. She enjoyed dressing up every day, applying her makeup, and donning flashy earrings. People stopped by her apartment daily to tease her and enjoy her teasing them.

In 1996, Mama's body began to deteriorate rapidly, and she had to enter the hospital. During her long stay, my sister and I experienced the pain of seeing our mother prepare for death as we too attempted to be ready to face the inevitable. Her body was broken down with abrasions. Her feet and legs suffered from sluggish circulation. She was unable to eat comfortably because of an apparent stroke. She couldn't move her body from her neck down without assistance. Yet we also experienced joy because she never lost her sense of humor. She never forgot how to sing the songs of the church. She never forgot how to pray. She never stopped watching or listening to Christian television. She didn't forget to celebrate her birthday.

The doctors told my sister and me that they marveled at the high pain tolerance Mama had. She never complained. But then, I'd never heard my mother complain about anything. She'd always say, "I hope so!" She never lost hope that things would improve.

Her tolerance of pain, lack of appetite, sore body, failing circulation, and long, quiet hours were signs that she was about ready to meet her Maker.

Sometimes I spent the night in her hospital room in the vacant bed next to her. I watched her for months, knowing in my heart that it wouldn't be long before my sister and I would be motherless. This really hit me one day as I watched her sleep. I wanted to ask her if she was ready to die, but I didn't know how. My daughter Lesa is so close to the Lord. I called her to ask her what I should do. "Just ask her!" Lesa said. "You know she's a Christian. Don't worry yourself! Find out how she's feeling about preparing to meet God."

I got up the nerve to ask her. "Mama, do you love the Lord?"

"Yes!" she answered.

"Are you ready to go where He is?"

"No!" she said emphatically.

When I told my sister about my exchange with Mama, we both interpreted her response as a sign that she might get well. She was always determined to get what she wanted! But within a few weeks her earthly determination turned to holy longing for her heavenly home. We saw it in her eyes, her smile, her soft speech.

I began to pray that God would take her home. She had suffered enough. We told the medical staff there would be no more surgeries. We did everything we could to make her comfortable.

I'll never forget the Thursday before her death. I stopped by the hospital on my way to choir rehearsal at church. She was sitting up in bed, watching television, teasing the staff, talking to some of the patients who came by to see her, eating, and having a good time. I hadn't seen her so beautiful in years. Her hair was shiny; her cheeks were rosy; her nails glistened with her favorite red polish. When I got to rehearsal, I reported that my mother was better that day than she had been in years. But I'd seen enough sickness to know the signs of death. I knew it wouldn't be long. I was right. Mama died three days later.

We honored Mama's life with a joyous home-going service. I read to the family these assurances about the death of a Christian:

- The death of a Christian is not the end of life, but a new beginning; death is not to be feared because it is a translation into another life. It is a release from the troubles of this world.

- The death of a Christian is precious in the sight of the Lord. It is a welcoming to a better place: our Father's house where there are many mansions and where we will receive a crown of righteousness. It is an entrance into peace and glory, into the presence of Christ.

- The death of a Christian assures rest and security, fellowship with other believers, activities of worship and singing, the ability to identify family members and friends who have gone to heaven.

- The consolation for Christians left in this world is that some day they too will be there to meet and greet their loved ones who have gone before.[1]

Death will always have its share of sorrow. We will always grieve when loved ones go on before us. But our grief can be less intense when we understand God's promises about eternal life with Him. All of us who love the Lord will experience a glorious transition when our mortal hearts stop beating. No wonder Mama liked to hear me sing to her during her last days. She especially loved "I'll Fly Away." Hallelujah!

Prayer

Dear Jesus, sometimes death is harsh and bitter, and I grieve the deaths of my loved ones. But I draw blessed peace from the fact that those who know and love You live on with You. Death isn't the end for those who know You as Savior and Lord. Thank You for Your Word, a source of great hope and comfort that calms my fear of death and gives me sweet hope for an eternal future. I can rest easy, knowing that when I leave this world, I will be safe in my Father's house with You. Amen.

God's Word to You

When the perishable has been clothed with the imperishable, and the mortal with immortality, then the saying that is written will come true: "Death has been swallowed up in victory."

"Where, O death, is your victory?
Where, O death, is your sting?"

The sting of death is sin, and the power of sin is the law. But thanks be to God! He gives us the victory through our Lord Jesus Christ (1 Corinthians 15:54-57).

Affirmation

I can rejoice even regarding death because Jesus has overcome it and given me eternal life with God.

30

Praying All the Time

I love to pray. I guess I'd better since I spend most of my time doing it! I wake up in the morning praying. I pray in the tub, I pray while I wash clothes and water the grass, I pray when I'm talking on the phone…hugging my children…driving…and exercising. I pray in meetings and during business negotiations. I pray on airplanes. I pray for the sick and the suffering and for people I don't know. Are you getting the picture? In almost every situation, my mouth isn't moving, but my brain is grooving. In my mind, I pray all the time.

One day as I was hugging my son goodbye after a visit, he said to me, "You're praying for me again, aren't you?" I looked a bit startled because I hadn't said a word about it aloud. I nodded my head. He said, "You're always praying. I can tell. You've done that since we were little. We all know it. But that's good, Mama. That's good. Thank you. Keep it up; don't stop now."

At other times, one of my children will call and ask, "Whatcha doin', praying?" My husband may walk into a room where I am and see me sitting very still, gazing into space. When I hear him turn to leave, I ask him what he wants. "Just wondering what you're doin'," he'll often say. "Were you praying?" And most of the time I am. I tend to pray when there's no apparent reason to pray. I just love to fellowship with my heavenly Father. What am I praying?

- "Lord, have mercy."

- "Help me, Lord."

- "Thank You, Jesus."
- "Speak to my heart, Lord."
- "Lord, are You listening?"
- "Lord, You know what I need; do it, please."
- "Help my children, Lord."
- "Put a hedge of protection around my family, Lord."
- "Guide my tongue, Sir."
- "God, why are You so slow?"
- "What's this all about, Jesus?"
- "Do You hear me, Lord?"
- "Am I supposed to keep asking You to do this, Sir?"
- "Look, Lord, I need an answer!"
- "Praise the name of Jesus."
- "I love You, Lord."

Some of those prayers may sound as if I'm a little sassy with God or disrespectful of Him, but the truth is, God is my Father and yours. He knows all about us. We can come boldly to Him, and He will understand exactly what we mean and the attitude with which we mean it. We can come clean with God. We can be ourselves with God. I don't know how your prayers sound, but I'm glad God can read our minds and know our hearts. When we realize that prayer is simply expressing our heart's sincere desire to God, in silence or aloud, prayer can become as natural as breathing.

When I'm in an attitude of prayer all the time, it's pretty hard to worry or to think of negative or evil things. People have asked me why I'm so happy all the time. I may not always be so happy, but I have joy in my heart! Such joy can come only in the presence of the Lord. This joy brings contentment when things are topsy-turvy. It calms my fears and smoothes my feathers and gives me peace when trials and tribulations are on the rampage. That joy surpasses all understanding as I trust in my Friend and Companion, Jesus.

Have you prayed today? Wherever you are and whatever you're doing, right now is a good time. You don't have to use theological lingo or flowery words. Just be yourself. God will understand exactly what you mean.

If you don't talk to Him every day, why not start now and make it a habit to talk to Him whenever you think about it? That must have been how I started praying so constantly. I just communicated with Him silently whenever He came to mind. I think that's what Paul, Silas, and Timothy meant when they urged the Thessalonians to "pray continually" (1 Thessalonians 5:17). Praying without ceasing involves abiding in the Father's presence, whether formal prayers are uttered or not.

God created us to have fellowship with Him. When we make a habit of talking to Him often, we make Him happy and He'll make us content. There is joy in the presence of the Lord!

Prayer

Father, I'm so glad You're always available. I can talk to You any time, day or night, no matter where I am or what I'm doing. I can talk to you about anything and everything. I don't have to hold back. I can even cry, yell, scream, laugh, giggle, and have fun with You. Thank You for accepting all my methods of getting in touch with You. It's good to know that whatever style I use, You're eternally ahead of me. You already know what I feel and need, and You've already solved the problem, answered the question, or handled the situation before I ask. What joy! Thank You for being so in touch with me. Amen.

God's Word to You

Evening, morning and noon I cry out in distress, and he hears my voice (Psalm 55:17).

Affirmation

I pray without ceasing because God wants to hear from me.

31

If Two of You Agree...

Something nasty was in the air on October 29, 1996. Three people in a row called me to report that either they were going into the hospital for breast cancer surgery or a loved one was. First, Marsha called to tell me she was scheduled for surgery on her breast that day. We prayed together that the surgery wouldn't be necessary—that God would perform surgery on her and heal her. I felt confident that our prayer would continue through my anointed friend Debra, who was going to be with Marsha. I've never in my life seen such unwavering faith as Debra has.

The next call came from my friend Peggy, whose daughter was scheduled for surgery that day. Peggy was distraught because she couldn't be there with Charlene, and she'd lost another daughter to cancer not many years before. Peggy and I prayed together that the Lord would watch over Charlene and that surgery would not be necessary. We also prayed that Charlene would not be upset that her mother couldn't be with her. We prayed that she would have complete and total healing and that God would be merciful and spare her life.

Another friend called later that morning to report that she was in the hospital getting prepped for surgery as we spoke. Shirley and I prayed that surgery wouldn't be necessary, but if she went through with it, there would be no complications and her suspected cancer would be benign and easily removed.

While waiting through the day to hear reports from my friends, I stood firm on God's Word: "Again, I tell you that if two of you on earth agree about anything you ask for, it will be done for you by my Father in heaven. For where two or three come together in my name, there am I with them" (Matthew 18:19). Jesus taught that there is great authority in corporate prayer. Where two or three who are committed to Christ pray in faith, He is in their midst. His presence imparts faith, strength, direction, peace, confidence, and grace. And He promises that when His children agree together according to His will, He will do what they ask.

At 2:30 that afternoon, Marsha phoned. I heard glee, joy, and excitement in her voice. She was back home from the hospital six hours after she'd checked in. The doctors had examined her breast in preparation for surgery, and guess what! They found nothing. Another doctor was sent in to confirm the original team's findings. The medical professionals didn't know what had happened, but they know what they saw on the original and subsequent X-rays. Whatever it was had vanished. Hallelujah! No surgery necessary. Marsha was released and told to see a doctor in six months.

Two more hours passed before I heard from Charlene, my friend Peggy's daughter. Again, good news. Charlene was also back home—no surgery necessary. Her doctor told her to go home until he could figure out what was happening. Apparently her condition didn't appear to be as serious as he'd thought. Again God had moved in a mysterious way.

Several days passed, and I didn't hear from my friend Shirley. On the following Sunday morning, I called Shirley's home to talk with her husband. She answered the telephone. She sounded out of it. But when she explained what had happened, there was again cause for rejoicing. Her tumor had been benign and was removed with no complications. However, the medication her doctor prescribed for pain was too strong or she didn't need it at all. The day before I called, she'd decided to discontinue the medication. What I heard in her voice was only the sluggishness caused by several days of being overmedicated.

God demonstrated His miracle-working power in all three of my friends' lives. Marsha still has no symptoms of cancer. Charlene has not needed breast surgery to this day. Shirley has completely recovered. These cases are extraordinary to me, but not to God.

Of course, God works in His own mysterious ways and doesn't always answer prayers so promptly. I have agreed and prayed with people and have waited days and months to see the manifestation of God's power through answered prayer. But while I've waited, I've experienced the peace and contentment of knowing He will answer in His time. Sometimes I tease Him and say it would be nice if He showed up early every now and then! But His timing is perfect. Healing my three friends during that short period of time was a part of God's master plan for their lives.

When you pray with other Christians, believing in faith, and God doesn't show up when you think He should, don't get discouraged. Many times I have prayed believing that my prayer was part of God's perfect will, yet He didn't move as quickly as I wanted Him to. One time I had to wait 16 years for Him to answer. But when He did, it was the right answer at the right time. While I was waiting on Him, I wondered what was happening. Sometimes I asked if He'd heard me. Was I praying right? What else could I do? But deep within He assured me that He would see me through. And He'll do the same for you.

Prayer

Father, standing together in Your midst is the most confident place to be. Thank You for loving Your children enough to show us the manifestation of Your goodness through answered prayer. As You honor my prayers, help me to honor and trust Your perfect, mysterious ways. Amen.

God's Word to You

This is the confidence we have in approaching God: that if we ask anything according to his will, he hears us. And if we know that he hears us—whatever we ask—we know that we have what we asked of him (1 John 5:14-15).

Affirmation

*When I pray with other Christians according to God's will,
I know our prayers will be answered.*

32

The Answer Book

When I was a little girl, my teachers at church would tell us that everything we wanted to know about was in the Bible. They told us the strange stories about Jonah being inside the whale; river waters parting and bunches of people walking through on dry land; Jesus feeding thousands of folks with a little bit of bread and fish; old man Noah building a huge boat and taking two of every land animal on it before the big rain. I was fascinated by the stories. But it wasn't until I became a teenager that I was forced by Mr. Beckett, my Sunday school teacher, to read the Bible myself because it really did give answers to all the questions I had.

Still, my love for studying the Bible didn't really blossom until after I married and started having major challenges in my life. I studied passages that dealt with what was going on at the moment—subjects such as forgiveness, work relationships, giving, family situations—and discovered that God's Word is as relevant today as it was thousands of years ago when it was written. And once biblical principles came alive in my mind and heart, I started practicing them, and they became my lifestyle. Now I can't get enough of reading the Bible! I want to be like the people in the synagogue in Berea: "These were more noble-minded than those in Thessalonica, for they received the word with great eagerness, examining the Scriptures daily to see whether these things were so" (Acts 17:11 NASB).

Studying the Scriptures is critical for any believer who wants to grow in knowledge and wisdom. In Hebrews 4:12-13 (NASB) we're told,

> For the word of God is living and active and sharper than any two-edged sword, and piercing as far as the division of soul and spirit, of both joints and marrow, and able to judge the thoughts and intentions of the heart. And there is no creature hidden from His sight, but all things are open and laid bare to the eyes of Him with whom we have to do.

It is enlightening to know the Bible has reflective power. It gives us the ability to see ourselves as God sees us. And when we see ourselves as sinners, we are told how to become clean and be received as members of the household of faith (Psalm 51; Ephesians 5:26-27). Our guide for all of life is the Bible. Jesus said,

> As the Father has loved me, so have I loved you. Now remain in my love. If you obey my commands, you will remain in my love, just as I have obeyed my Father's commands and remain in his love. I have told you this so that my joy may be in you and that your joy may be complete (John 15:9-12).

Psalm 119:105 says God's Word "is a lamp to my feet and a light for my path."

Do you have questions lurking in the back of your mind? Questions you don't want to ask anybody or questions you've asked but haven't gotten satisfactory answers to? Let me recommend prayerful study of the Bible. When you pray and ask for clarity before you study, you'll be amazed at how God reveals to you just what you need at that particular time. He knows what you need before you do!

If you're not a regular Bible reader, I invite you to catch the excitement with me and thousands of others. Start a little at a time. Or think of a topic you want to know more about, and start with that. I guarantee you'll get enthused by what you'll learn, and someone will have to pry you away from your reading so you can go to bed. There's no better book in the world than the Word of God.

Prayer

Dear God, You gave brilliant men the ability to write Your inspired Word so that people throughout the world can read, study, and understand more about You. Thank You for making Your Word so relevant to my life today. And thank You for the gift of communication with You. I don't have to second-guess You. I can ask You and study Your Word. Help me to remember that the rewards of knowing Your Word are great. Amen.

God's Word to You

The law of the LORD is perfect, reviving the soul.
The statutes of the LORD are trustworthy, making wise the
simple.
The precepts of the LORD are right, giving joy to the heart.
The commands of the LORD are radiant, giving light to the
eyes.
The fear of the LORD is pure, enduring forever.
The ordinances of the LORD are sure and altogether
righteous.
They are more precious than gold, than much pure gold;
they are sweeter than honey, than honey from the comb.
By them is your servant warned; in keeping them there is
great reward (Psalm 19:7-11).

Affirmation

*As a faithful student of the Bible, I am rewarded
with growing knowledge, wisdom, and character.*

33

You Shall Not Lie

I f there was one thing Granny hated more than anything, it was being lied to. When I lied, I made her the maddest. I could never figure out how she knew, but she could always tell when I wasn't being truthful. She told me she had eyes in the back of her head, and I believed her! She told me she could look through muddy water and see the bottom, and I believed that too. Somehow she always knew what was going on. Now that I have children of my own, I have a better understanding of her intuition.

I'll never forget the time in kindergarten when I stole a dime. Well, I didn't consider it stealing; it was lying there and I just picked it up. When I got home with a dime Granny knew I hadn't left home with, she asked me where I got it. I told her I found it. She interrogated me about where I found it, if I'd told the teacher I found it, how long I'd had it, why I didn't tell her about it as soon as I got home, and so on. Her interrogation seemed to last a lifetime.

Granny had a way about her when she thought someone was lying. She'd do the silent treatment thing until the truth came out. After I said I found the dime, she just looked at me strangely all evening, holding her thin brown lips tightly together—as if loosening them would accidentally let a word slip out.

The next morning she was up bright and early, and I woke to her standing over me and my bed. She looked like a giant. Her eyes were wide and questioning. She parted those thin, tight lips, and with a soft-but-frightening voice asked me again, "Where did you get that dime? Don't you lie to me. If it's one thing I can't stand, it's a liar!" I was in real trouble now! I knew I had to face the music eventually, so I said, "I took it off the table at school." To which she replied, "Get up. Put your clothes on. I'm going to school with you this morning. You will stand up before the class and tell them you stole a dime and you are sorry. You will apologize to your teacher and tell her you will never do that again. And when you come home, I'm going to whip you for lying. If you had told me the truth, you might have been punished once. But now you'll get two punishments: one for stealing and one for lying. Girl, don't you know that if you'll lie, you'll steal, and if you'll steal, you'll kill? I will not have a lying, thieving killer in my house! You will not lie to me and live! I love you too much to see you grow up to be a liar. It hurts me to have to do this to you, but you will learn not to lie. Do you hear me? Do you understand, Girl?"

"Yes, ma'am, I sure do." By the time she finished fussing with me, I wished she'd kept those tight lips tight.

The day went just as she planned. We got to school where she ushered me directly to my teacher, and I told her what I had done. Granny insisted that I needed to make a statement in front of the class when they assembled. With tears of humiliation streaming down my face I said to my peers, "I'm sorry I stole a dime yesterday. I won't do it again." I don't remember how my classmates reacted; I just remember promising myself I would never be in that situation again!

When I got home that afternoon, there was Granny sitting in her favorite spot in the corner of that ugly brown velveteen couch. In her hand was a switch with three limbs platted together from off the old nonbearing mulberry tree in the front yard. She told me to come on in. She was going to whip lying out of me that day.

You would think I'd have learned the lesson of a lifetime from that incident, but apparently I didn't because I remember another time I got caught lying to Granny. I was about nine years old and had just been released from Children's Medical Center in Dallas. I'd been in the hospital because I was too fat. Fat had surrounded my heart, causing some medical conditions that were correctable only by losing weight. Within ten days in the hospital the doctors had reduced me to a normal weight for a child my age. When I was released to go home, I had to remain on the diet for months until my metabolism became regulated and my eating habits changed for good.

Patty, the little girl who lived next door to us, was out playing in the yard one day shortly after I got home. Granny let me go over to play with her. While we were playing, Patty was eating a Hershey bar. It looked so good. I ate one bite. Surely that wouldn't harm me. I held the chocolate in my mouth without swallowing it for as long as I could. I didn't realize that chocolate residue pooled visibly in the corners of my mouth.

When I went back home, Granny asked me what I'd had to eat.

"Nothing," I lied.

She pointedly asked if I'd eaten any candy.

"No."

"Then what's that in the corners of your mouth?"

I replied innocently, "I don't know."

We went on like that for a little while. Then Granny let loose. I got severely fussed at about lying again, and then she cut some switches from the mulberry tree. Need I say more? The whipping and scolding went on for hours, it seemed. I heard the same lecture about lying and stealing and killing. Granny got her point across. I finally learned that a person's word is her bond. If I wasn't honest, I couldn't be trusted.

The fact that one of the Ten Commandments is "You shall not give false testimony" means that lying is neither a necessity nor an option (Exodus 20:16). We don't have to lie, and we have no excuse for lying. Granny did me a favor by lecturing me and punishing me when I lied to her. She instilled in me the principle that honesty is always the best policy. This principle has guided me throughout my career, with my family, and in all my relationships. God's commands make sense. Telling the truth is sure a lot easier than having to cover my tracks or face the righteous anger of Granny!

Prayer

Father, You never ask us to do anything without equipping us to do it. So when You told us not to lie, You gave us the ability to tell the truth always. Help me to remember that You are the truth and that being Your child means I have Your spiritual DNA. Your Son's blood covers me and enables me to do Your will. Thank You for Your loving discipline that helps rid my life of all deceit. Amen.

God's Word to You

My son, do not make light of the Lord's discipline, and do not lose heart when he rebukes you, because the Lord disciplines those he loves, and he punishes everyone he accepts as a son (Hebrews 12:5-6).

Affirmation

*I welcome God's discipline because I know
it is evidence of His love for me.*

34

No Lone Rangers

Judy and I worked together on the Dallas Institute of Banking board of directors years ago. I was a director; Judy was the administrator. Not being able to see the future, I had no idea that the Lord was planting a person in my life who would be a wonderful source of creativity for my speaking business many years later. In fact, back then I never thought of Judy as a creative person. We never had that kind of interaction.

A couple of years ago, after I had my own business and had hired Judy, we were together in my office brainstorming about things that could bring money into the business and help finance my television program. Watching and listening to Judy, I suddenly discovered a different person. The person I'd known was the corporate executive who was building an organization from a meager beginning to a thriving operation. The person sitting in my office now was a sensitive wife, mother, grandmother, businesswoman, and creative genius. Judy is an organizer, strategist, analyst, creator, and implementer of workable ideas—ideas that included creating a ministering postcard, greeting cards, pocket cards, T-shirts, and other products that would benefit people and honor God.

God has prepared everybody and everything we need to carry out His will for our lives. To each of us, He gives the particular talents He wants us to have, and He plants us in one another's paths to assist in accomplishing what He wants us to do. The fact that no man or woman is an island is evident when we look around at all the people who help us succeed. I can't count the many people who have been instrumental in my success. I could never have done it on my own! Nor did God want me to…and He still doesn't.

I can't help thinking about the time I was determined to play the piano. I knew God would allow me to learn to play like my talented friend, Dr. Shirley Gregory Harris. But piano lessons were drudgery. I struggled and struggled with those lessons. I sat at my piano for hours trying to make music come out of it. No music ever came…but noise did. I even bought a new piano, thinking that something was wrong with the first one. But nothing was wrong with the piano; something was wrong with the pianist! I had absolutely no aptitude to play an instrument of any kind. The sad thing about me and my piano struggle is that even though I loved my friend Shirley, I didn't like the idea that she could play and I couldn't. I envied her.

Finally, after three years of torturing myself with constant practice, the lightbulb came on. I thought, *Silly girl, God did not give you the gift of piano playing. He gave you the gift of singing and speaking. He gave Shirley the blessed gift of playing the piano. Get that through your thick head! Shirley can't sing; you can. You can't play; Shirley can. Wouldn't it be logical to ask her to play for you when you sing? God has given all of us gifts to magnify Him with. Why are you cutting off your blessing by envying someone's God-given gift? Get a grip!*

So I went to the telephone and called Shirley. I said, "The next time I sing, will you play for me?" Shirley replied, "Thelma Lou, I've been waiting on you to ask. Sure, I will. The Lord bless you, child!" Ever since that day more than 20 years ago, Shirley and I have presented music together, and God has blessed people and us through this ministry of sharing the gift of praise and exhortation. Isn't He amazing?

The Bible tells us that each of us is given gifts:

> Now to each one the manifestation of the Spirit is given for the common good. To one there is given through the Spirit the message of wisdom, to another the message of knowledge by means of the same Spirit, to another faith by the same Spirit, to another gifts of healing by that one Spirit, to another miraculous powers, to another prophecy, to another distinguishing between spirits, to another speaking in different kinds of tongues, and to still another the interpretation of tongues. All these are the work of one and the same Spirit, and he gives them to each one, just as he determines (1 Corinthians 12:7-11).

And Ephesians 4:11-13 instructs,

> It was [Christ] who gave some to be apostles, some to be prophets, some to be evangelists, and some to be pastors and teachers, to prepare God's people for works of service, so that the body of Christ may be built up until we all reach unity in the faith and in the knowledge of the Son of God and become mature, attaining to the whole measure of the fullness of Christ.

God uses all of us to accomplish His purposes. He established His body in such a way that no one person has all it takes to fulfill every ministry and mission on this earth. God's children must work as a team.

God knew before I was born what He had for me to do and who would help me. At every juncture, He supplies the people, places, products, and all the pieces I need to help me carry out His plans. Judy is one of those powerful pieces. Moses had his brother, sister, father-in-law, and tribal leaders who helped him manage the children of Israel. Paul had Barnabas and Timothy to help keep the churches together. Jesus had His disciples; and He instructed them to carry the good news of the gospel to everyone. He also had His inner circle of brethren whom He depended on to assist in His great camp meetings. Even God Almighty in Jesus Christ didn't try to be a lone ranger.

Consider the people who have helped you become the person you are and those who are in your corner pushing and encouraging you now. They have different interests, skills, abilities, and expertise from what you possess. Isn't it encouraging who God has put in your path? I'm amazed to see how God gives every person attributes that are distinct from everyone else's. There are billions of people all over the world, yet God makes them all different. Our uniqueness is so satisfying when we are willing to join together to the glory of God.

Prayer

Father, You demonstrated Your creative powers when You put order to a world that was without form. And when You created humankind, You made sure that no two people would be alike. That blows my mind! Thank You for providing everything I need when I need it to accomplish the tasks You've assigned me. Remind me not to be a lone ranger, but to celebrate and use every person's gifts in my efforts to further Your kingdom. Amen.

God's Word to You

Just as each of us has one body with many members, and these members do not all have the same function, so in Christ we who are many form one body, and each member belongs to all the others (Romans 12:4-5).

Affirmation

*As a member of the body of Christ, I have
a unique role to fulfill—
and so does everyone else.*

35

Ode to Mrs. Taylor

Helping customers at the bank where I worked was a pleasure. I was gratified to see them come in disturbed about something and leave with smiles of satisfaction. I told the people I supervised to emphasize to customers, whenever possible, what we can do because they weren't interested in what we couldn't do.

Early one Monday morning, Mrs. Taylor came into the department ranting and raving, as mad as a wet hen. She demanded that the customer service women do something they couldn't do. They were very professional and carefully explained what Mrs. Taylor's options were, but she didn't like any of her choices. Several times they tried to reason with her but to no avail. They knew they could come and get me if they couldn't solve a problem or handle a person, so they eventually did.

I approached Mrs. Taylor and calmly explained what we *could* do to help. It wasn't good enough. I've never seen anyone so irate. She kept yelling at the top of her lungs. She was so angry that she cussed at me for everything she could think of. I kept eye contact and maintained a look of sincere understanding. I let her vent.

When she finished, I explained that I understood how she could be so upset about her situation. However... And then I repeated what I'd already told her. (That's called the "Broken Record Method.") Mrs. Taylor became even more irate and started gesturing with her hands, fingers, elbows, fists, and other auspicious parts of her anatomy while adding new cuss words to her tirade. All the time she was going on and on, people who thought they wanted something out of their safe-deposit boxes decided they didn't need anything. They stopped to watch the action. People who were en route to the break room decided they didn't need a break. They stopped to see the show. A lot of people were entertained that morning by the drama put on by Mrs. Taylor.

She finally headed toward the elevator and left without being satisfied. I went back to my office content we had done all we could to assist her. I was pleased that I'd exercised self-control in handling the explosive situation. A gentleman who observed most of the action asked me, "Madam, how could you stand there and take that from that woman? I would have pulled her over the counter." My response? "Sir, I was doing everything I could to help her. I wasn't going to go down to her level. I'm not any of 'those people' like she called me. I know who I am!"

Six years later (not months, but years), I was teaching a course at the American National Bank in Austin, Texas. Guess who was there? Yep, Mrs. Taylor. She came to me during the break and asked me if I knew who she was. Honestly, I'd forgotten what she looked like. I did, however, recognize her name. She explained to me what had happened that long-ago day: "The day I was in the bank, my husband and I had lost everything we had. Since then we've moved to a small town near Austin to start over again. I'm now a teller in a bank." That was her way of vindicating herself, of saying she was sorry. We had a brief but friendly talk.

Can you imagine how Mrs. Taylor must have felt when she thought about how she acted that day? She wasn't a bad or nasty person. She was a frightened, embarrassed, humiliated person feeling out of control. As I look back to that day, I'm so glad God gave me the choice of losing my cool or maintaining control. I chose to be empathetic and compassionate and not retaliate when Mrs. Taylor was calling me names. I could have justified getting upset and reciprocating her attitude, especially when she talked ugly about my mother. But I didn't, thanks to God! You see, I've never lost a business, home, car, and everything I own. I don't know how I'd act if that were to happen to me. I can only say how I hope I'd act. I've lived long enough to never say "never."

Flying off the handle with people is not the response Jesus would use. As Christians, we are expected to bear the fruit of the Holy Spirit. When we accept Christ as our personal Savior, the Holy Spirit dwells in us and manifests His fruit in our lives. One result is self-control. When Mrs. Taylor was disrespecting me, something within me—the Holy Spirit—kept me from getting angry at her. I never felt the desire to be mean to her. All I wanted to do was help.

Another fruit of the Spirit is love. The only way we can fulfill the will of God in our lives is to be love-inspired, love-mastered, and love-driven. A person controlled by the Holy Spirit needs no law to cause her to live a righteous life. I imagine we've all been in situations where self-control was difficult to maintain, but we will bear the fruit of God's Spirit if we surrender to Him.

Prayer

Father, what a joy to have the Holy Spirit reside within me. Because the Spirit is aware of all things, He guides me into all truth. And that includes showing me how to respond to others in love, especially if he or she is doing or saying unkind things to me. Lord, I trust You to manifest Your spiritual fruit in me in every situation. Amen.

God's Word to You

The fruit of the Spirit is love, joy, peace, patience, kindness, goodness, faithfulness, gentleness, self-control. Against such things there is no law. Those who belong to Christ Jesus have crucified the sinful nature with its passions and desires (Galatians 5:22-24).

Affirmation

The fruit of the Spirit grows in me because I belong to Christ.

Go and Make Disciples

A lot of times I find myself dodging my responsibility to witness to people who may not know Jesus. You know…the person bagging groceries at the store, the taxi driver who takes me to my hotel, the hotel reception-ist, a business client, an acquaintance at the beauty shop, an attendant at the service station. But for Christians, the charge we're given by Jesus isn't optional…and it does come with a promise: "Go and make disciples of all nations, baptizing them in the name of the Father and of the Son and of the Holy Spirit, and teaching them to obey everything I have commanded you. And surely I am with you always, to the very end of the age" (Matthew 28:19-20).

This security from God is promised to us when we bear witness, winning the lost to Christ and teaching them to obey His righteous standards. It's comforting to know that whether we are weak, strong, reluctant, forceful, shy, assertive, covert, overt, bound, or free in presenting Christ to people, He never leaves us by ourselves. Jesus is alive and present in each of His children in the person of the Holy Spirit. He emboldens us to share the gospel.

The good news of the gospel is that Jesus Christ was born, was crucified, and rose again so that every person can experience eternal life with Him…if they choose to. God sent His only Son to die on a cruel cross so that we could be saved from our sins and be restored to an intimate relationship with Him.

People in the Old Testament days who recognized God as Creator, sov-ereign Lord, and accepted His authority as their Master were saved. Faithful people such as Jeremiah, Joel, Abraham, Isaac, and Jacob are going to be in heaven with us. All the Old Testament writers were saved under the dispensation of the Law. But after Christ came, the Law became alive in Him because He came to fulfill the Law. After He died on Calvary's cross and rose on the third day, conquering death and hell, a new dispensation called "grace" was ushered in. Now we can tell the truly good news that the kingdom of heaven has come to earth in the form of Jesus to wash away sin in all who will receive Him. The Bible assures us, "For God so loved the world that He gave His only begotten Son, that whoever believes in Him should not perish but have everlasting life" (John 3:16 NKJV).

Scripture spells out three specific requirements for salvation under grace:

- Confession that we are sinners. We must recognize that our sinful condition separates us from God.

- Belief that Jesus is the Christ and Messiah, sent by God to die for our sins.

- Faith that God raised Jesus from the dead to reign forever as Lord of our lives and King of the universe.

Salvation is the first step in becoming a practicing Christian. After that, just like a baby, a person has to be nurtured and trained toward maturity.

Sometimes this salvation business can be confusing because so many people have different opinions. Some believe that a person has to stop doing any kind of wrong before she can receive salvation. Others think they can do enough good works, such as helping people and being kind, to earn salvation. Still others think that because they were raised in a religious home, they are automatically saved. Scripture clearly teaches that salvation is a personal relationship with God granted only to those who sincerely ask Christ into their hearts and believe by faith what the Scriptures say about Him.

The New Testament has more than 40 scriptures about effective witnessing. I suppose the two things that make Christians most reluctant to witness are the fear of rejection and the uncertainty of what to say and how to say it. I use a variety of methods to be a more effective soul winner:

- Passing out or mailing a copy of my personally designed postcard, which carries a simple message of my love for Christ.

- Passing out pocket cards with a message of hope on them.

- Asking people if they are saved and explaining what I mean to those who don't have a clue.

- Guiding people in making decisions by giving them biblical principles and scriptures to read.

- Answering my mail and including the plan of salvation and/or other encouraging passages of Scripture.

- Giving complimentary books, bookmarks, or other gifts that point to Jesus.

- Inviting people to a Christian play or outing.

- Wearing a Christian T-shirt or other articles of clothing or jewelry.

- Carrying and reading my Bible in public.

- Singing gospel music.

- Reciting scriptures or Christian principles in my seminars or in general conversation.

- Treating people with a servant's heart of love. "They will know we are Christians by our love."[1]

I've discovered that God can use the simplest action, motivated by love, to fulfill His Great Commission through us. Perhaps the clearest evidence of salvation is living the kind of lifestyle Jesus would live if He were here today. One of the best statements about Christianity I've heard was made by a woman evangelist I greatly respect: "Christianity is not a religion like most people think. Christianity is a life of imitating Jesus."

Ultimately God draws people to His Son. He will perfect (complete) what we have begun in Him. Our responsibility is to go in love and tell everyone within our reach about Jesus!

Prayer

Lord, please forgive me when I am lax in sharing the good news about You. Give me greater boldness to tell people about the salvation that can be theirs through faith in You. Thank You for promising to be with me when I witness for You and for helping me imitate You to the world. Amen.

God's Word to You

And [Jesus] said to them, "Go into all the world and preach the gospel to every creature" (Mark 16:15 NKJV).

Affirmation

*I have confidence that God is with me
when I talk to people about Him.*

37

I'll Never Teach Sunday School!

Ruby Rhone had just become general superintendent of the Sunday school program at our church. She noticed that women between the ages of 35 and 55 were seldom attending. Her goal was to offer the opportunity to study God's Word to all age-groups in the church, but somehow that particular group had fallen by the wayside because there was no teacher. Ruby knew that many of us who were members of the church were in the choir and did usher duties on Sundays. So why weren't we in Sunday school?

I'd attended Sunday school throughout my childhood. Regular church and Sunday school attendance were a given in my family. When I grew up and married, I said I'd never go to Sunday school again. I'd had my fill. *Let the children go because they need Sunday school,* I thought. *I don't.* Anyway, Sunday school was too early in the morning. I needed to rest because I worked all week, and I wanted time to do what I wanted to do. And that definitely did not include Sunday school.

Ruby called to nag me almost every week about starting the new Sunday school class. She knew I was a speaker and quite influential with many of the women in that age bracket at our church, which included most of my friends. Ruby had a dream, and I was one of the characters in it. Every time she asked me to please be the teacher, I told her, "No, thank you!" reasoning that Sunday morning was the only time I had to spend quality time with my husband. Her response? "He needs to be in Sunday school too!"

How long can a person be refused? Until she gets the response she wants.

My eventual response, after several months of her badgering, was that I wouldn't be the teacher, but I would come to the class sometimes. At that point, she'd gotten a commitment from five of us to attend the class and had found someone else to teach it. The six of us in attendance that next Sunday formed the "Truth Seekers Class."

The lessons were eye-opening, the discussions stimulating, the fellowship fulfilling. Every person brought something into the class that seemed to make it more complete and worthwhile. I started looking forward to Sunday mornings! My obvious enthusiasm prompted Ruby to start nagging me about becoming an assistant teacher. Finally I agreed. (I didn't admit I was a bit excited!)

Little did I know that Ruby had plans to promote the Truth Seekers current teacher and give me full responsibility for teaching the class. I found that out in the next month's conference for Sunday school workers. As the assistant teacher, I was the next in line to become the teacher. Ruby had won!

One of my best experiences is being the teacher of that class. Members include science teachers, college professors and other educators, engineers, and medical professionals who challenge me to prove the truth of everything I teach. Corporate executives and employees and government workers add their insights. Childcare workers, homemakers, and volunteers express their nurturing skills. Entrepreneurs, who often tend to be control addicts, love to try to take over or steer discussions. The atmosphere is wonderful! I interact with women from all walks of life, teach the Bible, and am challenged to study the lessons carefully to avoid embarrassment when they ask me hard questions.

These years of teaching the Truth Seekers have been the most enlightening years of my life. I didn't realize when I accepted this responsibility that I would grow from it much more than the rest of the class. I also didn't realize how much I did *not* know about the Word of God. I didn't realize just how much the affiliation with these women would enhance my life.

The original class of 5 has grown to 55. We're close enough to one another that when one member is hurting, the group feels the pain and offers to help. We've lent financial stability to the prison ministry that three of our members are active in each month. One of our members quit her teaching job to follow her calling as a foster mother. She and her family have lovingly cared for a number of children in their home. The Truth Seekers have been in prayer with her and her family during health crises and court cases and have witnessed the Lord's grace in healing a "crack baby" from the devastating effects of cocaine. Many of us have lost parents and other loved ones during the past few years. We have comforted one another.

Some mothers have watched their children stray from their Christian upbringing and pursue drugs, alcohol, and crime. We've been there for the parents, supporting and praying for them and theirs through the dark days. We've upheld those who are caring for aged parents or relatives.

We've celebrated birthdays, anniversaries, children's weddings, and births together. Many of us have vacationed together. The most joyful time we have together is Sunday morning when we praise the Lord with songs and prayers before we study the lesson. We are in one accord, praising God for His grace and mercy because He has brought us through the week and allowed us to assemble together again to edify one another and glorify Him.

Do you see what I would have missed if I'd continued to refuse to be a Sunday school teacher? My life would be void of this kind of fellowship and these relationships. I discovered that teaching a Sunday school class wasn't just standing before a group and demonstrating an ability to teach. Teaching is also the ability to share wisdom from the Word while demonstrating compassion and care for women who need support and fellowship as much as I do. A high point of my week is being with the Truth Seekers.

God has given all of us a ministry, whether we know it yet or not. Some of us are gifted teachers; others may be nurturers, peacemakers, writers, artists, singers, decorators, floral designers, musicians, and so forth. Whatever we get the most pleasure out of sharing with others can be a ministry tool in God's hands. Whatever encourages human beings and glorifies God is blessed by God. What ministry does He want to bless in your life today?

Prayer

Father, thank You for being patient with me. When You give me a ministry opportunity and I don't take it, keep tugging at my heart. Give me the desire to do what You have for me to do. Amen.

God's Word to You

Each one should use whatever gift he has received to serve others, faithfully administering God's grace in its various forms. If anyone speaks, he should do it as one speaking the very words of God. If anyone serves, he should do it with the strength God provides, so that in all things God may be praised through Jesus Christ. To him be the glory and the power for ever and ever. Amen (1 Peter 4:10-11).

Affirmation

When I am open to God's will, He shows me how
He wants to use me. He blesses my work for Him.

38

Until He Was Seven

A friend told me an interesting story about God removing our guilt.

Ann and her husband, Jim, noticed that their son, Tyrone, was spending a great deal of time and money on a little boy who must live in their neighborhood. He bought the child a bicycle for his birthday, and he often took the little boy riding with him.

Being a mother, my friend was proud of the time her son was taking with this little boy who obviously didn't have a father active in his life. *What a noble and worthwhile cause,* she thought.

Then one day Tyrone shared a secret with his parents. He couldn't bear to keep quiet any longer. He told his parents that from the time the child was three years old, they'd had a clandestine father–son relationship. Tyrone had attempted to be a part of the little boy's immediate family, but the child's mother wouldn't allow it.

"We were both teenagers when Brenda had our son," Tyrone explained. "When she told me about the pregnancy, I panicked. How would I tell you I was going to be a father? I reacted poorly, and she took it personally. She decided that if I wouldn't share in the responsibility of our baby, I could not, in any way, be a part of their lives. Even when I came to my senses and tried to apologize and make up, she wouldn't have anything to do with me. Finally, three years after Troy's birth, she allowed me to come around to see him. I was elated, but it was heartbreaking too. I missed seeing my son all the time. I wanted his mother for my wife. That was the most difficult

153

time of my teenage life. I had come from a happy family where there were a mother and father, and I wanted the same thing for my child."

By the time Troy was ready to start elementary school, Tyrone had gotten so attached to his son that he didn't want to share him with anybody else. He felt he had missed his earlier years, and if other family members came into the picture, he would lose his place in line with Troy. But the older little Troy got, the more questions he asked. He wanted to know who he really was. Where had he come from? Who were his grandparents? Where were his other relatives?

Tyrone wondered, *How do you tell your mother and father they have a grandson? He's seven years old and already in school!* But he found the courage to tell them the truth, and a meeting was arranged. When Troy was introduced to the family, he knew all of them by name. Tyrone had shown him pictures and told Troy a lot about them. It was love at first sight: He liked them, and they loved him. Ann said, "I'll always remember that day. When Tyrone started to say, 'This is your Aunt…' Troy interrupted with 'Sharon!' He did the same with his Aunt Debra and with me. And then he looked at his grandfather and said, 'I know who this is. This is Big Daddy Jim!' Ann looked at her husband, who was trying to keep back the tears. "Big Daddy" is what Tyrone had affectionately called her husband's daddy, his grandfather.

Ann immediately started a ritual of rubbing Troy's head and giving him a big hug, and that has continued through the years. The only problem is that Troy is now very tall, and she's only five feet tall. Now she catches him around the waist, looks up, and asks, "How's the weather up there?" He always looks down at her with his boyish grin and big, bright eyes and says affectionately, "It's all right. How are you, Grandmother? Love ya!"

What a happy ending. The parents finally knew the truth about their son's little friend. He was their grandchild. All they regret is that they weren't a part of his life earlier. But God joined the two families together in due season. And even though Tyrone and Brenda are each married to other people, their spouses are wonderfully accepting and cooperative in blending the families. Troy has two brothers from his mother's marriage and two sisters from his father's marriage. Ann and Jim feel their family is complete because they have the blessing of enjoying all their grandchildren.

Today Troy is 16 and has two more years to go in public school. He says he wants to be a policeman. That's a good thing. Debra's husband is a policeman, his brother is a policeman, and some of their friends are police. Troy has a lot of role models and a lot of love.

Perhaps you've made a mistake that caused you or someone else guilt and pain. Can you imagine the agony of keeping a secret the way Tyrone did for seven years? You don't have to live with silent, private guilt! There are people who will listen with understanding. There are resources and agencies where people are trained to give professional advice. And God is always ready with His grace, mercy, and helping hand. He'll lift you out of guilt and shame and show you solutions to your problems.

Whatever may have happened in your past is over and done with. It's history. You can pack your guilt and shame away in a box, use duct tape around all the edges to seal it tightly, and put it in the trash where it belongs. Don't let the situation haunt you any longer. Why? Because Jesus cares about what happened in your past. And He cares even more about what you're doing today to recover from it. He wants you to bring your pain and shame to Him so He can fulfill His promise to you by forgiving you, cleansing you, and giving you His joy.

God brought indescribable joy out of a teenager's moral mistake. He gave peace to Tyrone after seven long years of guilt and shame. And He gave Ann and Jim a precious grandson named Troy. And God doesn't love that family any more than He loves you. Take your burden to Jesus! He loves you!

Prayer

Father, thank You for making it so I don't have to bear guilt and shame. You are always here to give me wise counsel even when I don't trust someone else with my secrets. Please show me someone I can trust to talk to about this situation. Thank You for providing a way for me to be cleansed of my guilt and receive Your joy. Amen.

God's Word to You

The Lord your God is gracious and merciful, and will not

turn His face from you if you return to Him (2 Chronicles 30:9 NKJV).

Affirmation

*I trust God to remove all my guilt
and shame and give me His joy.*

39

Low Self-esteem?

At one time or another, everybody experiences cycles of low self-esteem. Feelings of poor self-worth can be brought about by conditional love, criticism, rejection, alienation, oppression, health problems, loss of a loved one, change, incompetence, threats, indecision, inadequate education, verbal or physical abuse, substance or alcohol misuse, religious oppression, social pressures, lack of organization, fear of failure or success, yielding to temptations, physical appearance, failures, regrets, poverty, phoniness, family and domestic challenges, financial dilemmas, backstabbing. Should I continue this list?

In my book *Bumblebees Fly Anyway,* I described what it feels like to have a serious bout with low self-esteem:

> A crisis of self-esteem cuts deep into the personality, slicing at every nerve that would try to tell you that you are valuable, worthwhile, and precious. It jabs and taunts with messages that say, "You'll never be anything. You'll never do anything significant. You're as necessary as dryer lint, and just about as attractive."[1]

Perhaps the things that cause your cycles of low self-esteem weren't listed, but you know what they are. Or you think you do. But guess what? In my opinion, the greatest cause of low self-esteem is simply not knowing who we are in Christ. When we don't understand our origin and how essential we are to the universal scheme of God's plan for this world, doubts about our worth result.

Signs of low self-esteem include:

- Grandiosity—the attempt to make people think everything we do or have is better than what everyone else does or has.

- Name-dropping—the attempt to make people think we are important by identifying the people with whom we have associations.

- Running away from obligations—being irresponsible.

- People pleasing—trying to please everybody all the time.

- Always apologizing—accepting blame for most things.

- Pessimism—constantly finding what's wrong in almost everything and everybody.

- Whining and complaining—often griping and playing the victim.

- Putting people down—gossiping maliciously.

- Oversensitivity—taking what people do and say personally when it may not be meant that way.

- Perfectionism—attempting to live up to impossible standards.

Many things can raise our self-esteem, including unconditional love, being appreciated, laughter, friendly and wholesome surroundings, being paid attention to, being listened to, compliments, accomplishments, reaching realistic goals, accepting our appearance unconditionally, appropriate touch, deep family connections, successful social and community affiliations, financial stability, contentment with where we are in our lives, fulfilling and gratifying activities, and taking time to relax and regroup. We need to realize, however, that whatever we do to feel better about ourselves is superficial without the true foundation of self-esteem and self-worth based on God's perfect love for us and the Holy Spirit's work in our lives. Without that solid backdrop, all our efforts and experiences will have temporary effects at best.

Occasionally I still have pity parties, but they last no longer than an hour. I won't permit them to go on too long. Sometimes I actually set my alarm clock to allow 15 minutes of unbridled self-beating. The alarm reminds me that I've spent enough time raking me over the coals and feeling down. When the situation seems really big, I might give myself up to an hour to feel bad. But that's plenty long enough. Part of me may want to stay in defeatist mode, but my spiritual side reminds me, "Hey, Thelma!

Don't you know who you are? You are a King's kid!" And so are you! You can take your situation to Him and ask Him to lift you out of this negative state and restore your gladness. Nothing has happened to you that God doesn't know about. He's already worked out the problem…all you have to do is ask for help! He loves you perfectly and completely. So get up, Girl! Pull yourself together. You are worth everything to God. That's why Jesus died for you, remember?

I've found two other practical, simple things to do that help me feel better when I'm doubting my self-worth: talk kindly to myself and smile. Yes, many low self-esteem problems arise from the way we talk to ourselves. When we tell ourselves we are worthless, ugly, clumsy, sick, incapable of doing anything right, that we can't do this or that, we look bad, and we're always victims, we can't help but feel unworthy of anything. Our thoughts and words have a powerful influence over us. To change how we're feeling, we must consciously choose to change what we tell ourselves.

That's one reason I've included an affirmation at the end of each reading in this book. This positive phrase is in present tense because it's true and ready to embrace. The affirmation for this devotion is, "I can always feel good about myself because of God's perfect love for me." This statement isn't arrogant, haughty, or deceitful. Rather, it is an expression of the fact that we can love ourselves with the kind of love embodied in Jesus Christ. Because God has made us in His image and loved us so much that He sent His only Son to die for us, it makes sense that we should love ourselves God's way. God even told us to love our enemies as we love ourselves. Let's not miss the point!

There may be times when, for whatever reason, you don't love yourself. If you want to feel better about yourself and acknowledge the truth, repeat this affirmation…or choose another one relevant to your situation. It will help. One of my favorite affirmations is straight from the Scriptures: "I can do all things through Christ who strengthens me" (Philippians 4:13 NKJV). Sometimes when I repeat this affirmation, I'm not doing all the things I can and should do. However, this verse reassures me that when I rely on the One who works through me to do all the things He wants me to do, I am whole and victorious.

Smiling is therapeutic as well. When I'm feeling sorry or sad, I remind myself to smile. I try to think of things that make me happy (such as my grandchildren!). Sometimes I read something funny, watch a comedy on television, or talk to somebody who makes me laugh. Smiling and laughing are good attitude adjusters. Our facial expressions tend to control how we feel about ourselves and those around us. People who smile as a lifestyle are less susceptible to anger, frustration, agitation, aggravation, and many other negative "-ations" that easily pull people down. People who seldom smile often feel angry, sad, and bad about themselves. People with positive self-esteem seem to...

- smile often
- seldom make excuses or run away from obligations
- look for the best in people
- take risks
- adapt well to change (flexibility)
- seldom talk negatively about people
- enjoy a wide variety of interests
- display an eagerness to learn
- keep an open mind
- pursue excellence rather than perfection

So much of how we feel depends on how we choose to think. We can decide to dislike ourselves or we can opt to enjoy ourselves the way we are. We can decide to have a pity party or skip that type of party and even refuse to go to someone else's. In fact, as Christians, we really don't have the option of having low self-esteem. Jesus paid for all our sins and faults so we don't have to beat ourselves up for what we've experienced or done. We can seek forgiveness and mercy and grace in Him...and He gladly bestows it.

The next time you feel bad about yourself and doubt your worth, follow King David's example and talk to God. Recite the truth of who you are:

> For you [God] created my inmost being; you knit me together in my mother's womb. I praise you because I am fearfully and wonderfully made; your works are wonderful, I know that full well. My frame was not hidden from you when I was made in the secret place. When I was woven together in the depths of the earth, your eyes saw my unformed body. All the days ordained for me were written

in your book before one of them came to be. How precious to me are your thoughts, O God! How vast is the sum of them! Were I to count them, they would outnumber the grains of sand. When I awake, I am still with you (Psalm 139:13-18).

God already knows who you are, of course, but you will feel better when you hear yourself telling Him. When you're aware of the value God places on you and of how perfectly He loves you (as only He can), low self-esteem will disappear. Praise His holy name!

Prayer

Father God, You chose to make me in Your image. You had me on Your mind when You formed the universe. I'm so thankful to You for not leaving me to battle low self-worth by myself. You have given me the knowledge and wisdom to understand that nothing can take away my precious heritage in You. Thank You for giving me Your Word and the assurance that I am worth everything to You. You love me so much that You have my name written on Your hands. Remind me often that I have great worth because of who I am in You. Amen.

God's Word to You

There is no fear in love. But perfect love drives out fear, because fear has to do with punishment. The one who fears is not made perfect in love (1 John 4:18).

Affirmation

I can always feel good about myself because of God's perfect love for me.

40

R-E-S-P-E-C-T

The flight from Singapore to Perth, Australia, turned out to be a free seminar for the gentleman sitting next to me. I'd just finished teaching a seminar in Singapore called "Negotiating Skills for Secretaries." It had been a challenging experience because, at that time at least, secretaries in that country were women who seldom had the option or opportunity of negotiating. They were expected to answer the telephone, take messages, work hard, and keep organized. Learning how to negotiate with their bosses wasn't high on their list of priorities (or their bosses' priorities). All day I'd reworked the seminar as I went along so the secretaries would find some truths and wisdom they could use to help them in their jobs.

When I got on the airplane, I decided I was going to interview someone who knew the Australian business atmosphere and what is generally expected of secretaries so I could avoid the blunders I'd made in Singapore and be better prepared. I like the aisle seat because it puts me at an advantage. If the person in the window seat gets annoyed with me, he or she has to talk to me to get up and move. Being in the aisle seat gives me some control of my seatmate's activities.

I gathered from his briefcase and attire that the gentleman sitting next to me was a businessman. As he fastened his seat belt, I asked his name. He hesitated a moment before telling me, but I was pleased to detect an Australian accent. I told him my name, which he clearly didn't care to know. While he adjusted his legal-sized yellow pad and got into position to write, I interrupted him. "What do you do?"

In a tone that clearly communicated "Leave me alone," he told me he was a district manager for a big outfit in Australia. I knew then he was my interview subject.

"Great!" I responded. "You're just the person I need to talk to." He wasn't a happy camper, but I continued. "I need to ask you some questions." I explained what I did for a living and briefly told him about my experience in Singapore. Then I asked, "Do you have a secretary?"

"Yes," he replied.

"What do you expect from your secretary?"

"What? What do I expect from my secretary?" he repeated.

"Yes."

After a few seconds with a "well, let me think about that" look on his face, he answered, "I expect her to outthink me."

"Oh? That's wonderful! And do you empower her to outthink you?" I asked.

He looked at me with disgust and asked, "What in the world are you talking about? What do you mean 'empower'?"

I was glad he asked! I explained that empowering means:

- giving people responsibility with accountability
- giving them ownership of projects and ideas
- allowing them to make decisions and supporting them in their decisions
- keeping them aware of what's going on in the company overall
- allowing them the freedom to do their jobs their way within established guidelines
- being a mentor and teaching them everything you know
- showing concern for their well-being
- giving them appropriate feedback and expecting the same from them
- showing appreciation for their work
- praising them when appropriate
- giving them credit for their ideas
- assisting them in advancing their careers

The man put his pen down, looked me in the eye, and said, "Look, lady, all this stuff about empowerment is a lot of baloney. People are hired to do a job. If they know what they're doing and get paid for it, you don't need to compliment them and praise them and help them all the time. If they can't do the job, they can get out. I'm not going to spend my time making people feel good. I want them to work!"

He didn't know it, but he was in for a free seminar. He had obviously planned to get back to that yellow pad, but I had other plans! I leaned toward him and asked him some more questions, giving him time to answer between each one:

- "Are you having much turnover in your company?"
- "How's the morale of the people who work for you?"
- "Are you experiencing a high volume of mistakes?"
- "Are people taking all their paid sick days?"
- "Do they work because they like working there or because they feel stuck there?"
- "Can you honestly say you're happy with the way things are going around your office?"

The guy put his pen down more gently this time and gave me his attention. He let me talk.

I explained to him there are four basic personality styles. These personality styles aren't right or wrong, good or bad—they're just the styles people tend to fall into during certain interactions. Each style is driven by certain goals and needs and is characterized by distinct behaviors and mannerisms. By understanding these styles, we can better work with and respect other people while helping bring out their best. Briefly I detailed these personality styles.

- *The Control Freak* or *Decision Maker.* This person is task oriented. He needs to be in charge, have his way, make decisions, avoid small talk, and get to the point with people. Sometimes he can be alienating and manipulative, but he can be depended on to get the job done.

     How do you deal with him effectively if your style is different? Remain businesslike. Don't beat around the bush when you have to tell him something. Don't waste his time with trivia when there is work to be done. Respect the fact that he knows what he's talking about most of the time. If you need to confront him, be sure you know what you're talking about. Time is important to him, so don't barge into his office unannounced and expect him to be polite and tactful. Don't take what he says or does too personally. At least you won't ever have to second-guess how he feels. This type of person doesn't need a lot of compliments. He knows he's good.

- *The Helpful Honey* or *Peacemaker*. This person is relationship ori-ented. She needs to feel wanted and appreciated. She is personable, kind, tender, committed, and concerned. She's the glue that holds things together but is easily intimidated by the Control Freak. She is often passive or passive-aggressive, meaning she holds her feelings inside until they get so bottled up she explodes. She has a memory like an elephant and will never forget anything you've done to her or for her. She operates best on compliments, appreciation, and support. If she makes you a promise, she'll do her best to keep it. Often she'll overextend herself in an effort to please and support other people.

  So how do you deal with her if your style is different? Give her a little time to talk. Ask her personal questions about her life and her family. Give her vocal approval of something she's done. Allow her the opportunity to set some priorities and make some decisions without criticism. She is capable of shouldering a lot of responsibility, but she may not solve a problem as quickly as the Control Freak will.

- *The Data Chip* or *Thinker*. This person is task oriented, but in a different way from the Control Freak. She needs to make sure that what she's supporting with her efforts is viable. She is pre-cise, organized, systematic, concise, and able to read between the lines. She can be unimaginative and resistant if she doesn't think a project can work. She may be described as the "no" person—the one who says no to most things until she's had an opportunity to analyze them, think about them, test them, and repeat the process several times. If you have a deadline and are expecting her to help you achieve it, you'd better make her deadline much more liberal than yours.

How do you deal with a Data Chip person if your style is different? Give her information in writing—not orally. Make sure your presentation is organized. When she gets it in writing, she can think through and analyze it without much delay. Disarray throws her into a quandary. Ask her for her opinion on an issue or project. She's usually already figured out the mistakes and loopholes, but she may not express what she knows until the project is underway or finished. Then she might say, "I knew all the time that it wasn't going to work, but nobody asked me."

- *The Attention-Getter* or *Enthusiast.* This person is relationship oriented, but different from the Helpful Honey. He needs to be noticed and is the life of any party. He is warm, polite, charismatic, articulate, often flashy, and a bit of a show-off. He may volunteer for a lot of things but do little in terms of actual work. One of the most positive attributes of the Attention-Getter is that he calls attention to other people so they get recognized too. This helps the group or team become more cohesive and more cooperative. He is also enthusiastic about projects, which often rubs off on the people he's working with. Unfortunately, at times he can be a good pretender. He enjoys taking the credit for a job well done when he actually delegated the job to someone else. Like the Control Freak, the Attention-Getter wants you to think he knows it all, but he is often only a superficial information gatherer.

  How do you deal with him effectively? Give him what he wants. Applaud him. Let him talk. Support his volunteerism but hold him accountable. Laugh at his jokes. Express your enthusiasm. What really discourages his enthusiasm is pessimism.

"Now, sir," I asked my seat partner, "which personality style do you exhibit most of the time?"

"I guess the first one," he said. "I don't need anybody wasting my time and beating around the bush. I can't stand to be around honey-dripping people. They irritate the heck out of me."

Our conversation had gotten serious. He was listening and agreeing with much of what I was saying. He admitted, "Maybe I've been a little too harsh. I never tell people when they're doing well. I never compliment people. I'm losing the best secretary I've ever had, and now I think it's because I never let her know how great she's doing. I've been told before that this isn't a good way to manage people, but I didn't really listen. Thank you for the information."

Then I hit him with the clincher: "What else did you learn from our conversation?" I felt comfortable asking because the chance of ever meeting him again was remote, and I didn't have a thing to lose. He calmly and gently said, "I've learned that people have their own way of acting and behaving, and everybody won't act like me or think like me. I must learn to respect other people's personality styles even if I don't like the way they do things if I want them to succeed and work effectively for me. It's going to be hard for me to practice this, but it's worth a try. My turnover rate is deplorable... and I think it's because of me."

Our conversation that began on the runway in Singapore came to a close at the gate in Perth. What had started out as an interview had turned into an impromptu discussion about the importance of respecting people's personality types. As I reflect on that interesting day, I think how important it is for everybody to understand how to deal with people on their wavelength. Much confusion and irritation in dealing with people would be minimized or eliminated if we'd only meet them where they are and respect their unique approaches to life and problem solving.

When the Bible talks about "respect," it refers to having high regard for others. We are to observe and discern the truth about people, show compassion and understanding, and behave with consideration so that the good qualities and attributes in them will be brought to the surface. Consideration and respect help and encourage people to blossom.

I was washing dishes one day while listening to Aretha Franklin singing her jivin' song "R-E-S-P-E-C-T." *That's exactly what people need from other people!* I thought. Employers need to respect their employees...and vice versa. Students need to respect their teachers and authority figures...and vice versa. Church members need to respect their ministers and religious leaders, and they need to be shown respect in return.

As God's representatives, we Christians should always demonstrate respect for everyone. As believers in Jesus, we are obligated to...

Regard each person as highly as we regard ourselves.

Extend a helping hand whenever needed.

Serve one another in love as Jesus did.

Protect one another from danger.

Evangelize the world.

Commit to helping others be their best.

Turn distrust into trust.

God expects us to respect one another. Psalm 145:8 asserts, "The Lord is gracious and full of compassion, slow to anger and great in mercy" (NKJV). If God can have compassion (respect, regard) for us, we can surely have compassion and respect for other people.

Are you in charge of other people's activities at work, school, home, or play? Making an effort to discover what makes them tick and what makes them act the way they do may decrease your stress, improve communication, and create a more productive work environment. In fact, it's actually fun to watch the interactions of different personality styles and see how they complement and balance one another. Every successful team needs a decision maker, a peacemaker, a thinker, and an enthusiast. God made all of us unique so that we can take up the slack and fill in the holes of life and circumstances with our distinct personalities. Let's appreciate and respect one another as He does.

Prayer

Father, You are so wise. You've given each of us individual per-sonalities. No two people are alike, although we do have some traits in common. I want to be a better observer of the people around me. Give me compassion and respect for other personality types, and help me work with them effectively. Let me encourage everyone I know to do his or her best. Thank You for modeling what consideration is all about. Amen.

God's Word to You

Then Peter began to speak: "I now realize how true it is that God does not show favoritism but accepts men from every nation who fear him and do what is right" (Acts 10:34-35).

Affirmation

*I will respect other people the way I want to be respected—
the way God respects each person.*

41

A Marriage Made in Heaven

On one of my trips from Athens, Georgia, to Atlanta, a woman introduced herself and told me she was on her way to get married for the third time. She said she had been sure that her second husband was the mate God had chosen for her, but evidently He had something else in store for her because her man had run around on her and she couldn't take it. She explained that he was a Christian, and both of them had worked in their church's children's ministry. He was a good father to their sons, but he just couldn't leave other women alone. He'd already married the last woman he'd left her for.

I thought a minute about what she'd said and responded, "No, ma'am, God didn't have different plans for you that caused your divorce. God never works in opposition to His plan for faithfulness in marriage. But Satan has a plan for every good thing God made. Because God ordained marriage as the first institution, and it was good, Satan does all he can to destroy the sanctity and purity of marriage. Don't blame God for your divorce. Put the blame where it belongs—on the devil."

I'm bewildered by how people can become so vulnerable that they allow the enemy to control them to the point of breaking their marriage vows. I also know, however, that there are weaknesses inside all of us that we must fight with the aid of the Holy Spirit. I imagine most married couples believe deep down that their marriages are forever. Most of them probably believe they are married to the mates God divinely prepared for them. And yet so many marriages are plagued with sexual infidelity, physical and psychological abuse, drug abuse and alcoholism, actual or emotional abandonment, and financial catastrophe. Whether these issues arise occasionally or frequently, they take their toll on the unions.

I truly believe that many marriages that have ended in divorce were marriages made in heaven. Satan, the enemy of God and His children, is a liar, schemer, and deceiver, and he takes pleasure in destroying what God has joined together. I encourage you to be diligent in prayer and fasting when troubles come. Jesus said to His disciples, "I tell you the truth, if you have faith as small as a mustard seed, you can say to this mountain, 'Move from here to there' and it will move. Nothing will be impossible for you" (Matthew 17:20). And He added that some things don't happen without "prayer and fasting" (Mark 9:29 NKJV). We need to persevere when we ask Him for help and healing.

My marriage has gone through tremendous trials and temptations. I married young—the day after my twentieth birthday. I entered marriage with the fairy tale idea of "living happily ever after." Little things, such as not going shopping together because George didn't like to window-shop, caused anger. I was frustrated that he left his shoes, socks, and underwear lying around and expected me to pick up after him. I didn't know that came with marriage! Larger things troubled me too, such as when George made major financial decisions without my input. (He once sold my favorite car without talking to me about it. It didn't matter that the buyers were his parents. I was his wife!) Even though we straightened that one out and it never happened again, I thought more than once, *This marriage stuff ain't all it's cracked up to be.*

More than 25 years ago, our situation got gigantic. George admitted to infidelity—the straw that almost broke the camel's back. I seriously considered divorce, but thanks be to God, the Lord sent help. We discovered that His grace is sufficient for all our needs, including putting a broken marriage back together. I will never forget the early morning phone call we received one Saturday. On the other end of the line were our friends C.L. Walker and his wife, Thelma.

"Are you up, Thelma?" Mr. Walker asked.

"No, sir," I answered.

"Well, wake up and put George on the phone too."

I obeyed.

"George and Thelma," Mr. Walker said, "I don't know what's going on in your house, but the Lord didn't let me sleep all night. He had me praying for and thinking about y'all. Whatever's happening, it's not good. God is not pleased, and the two of you had better get it straight. My wife and I want to pray for you right now." Mr. and Mrs. Walker then prayed words of admonition to us and petitioned God for our unity, decisions, peace, and problem solving. I couldn't believe somebody was praying for us! The Walkers knew nothing about our problems; we had confided in no one at that time. There was no doubt in our minds that the Holy Spirit had prompted them to call us.

After that prayer, my husband and I went back to bed, but neither of us could go back to sleep. We lay completely silent except for the intense breathing and intermittent sobbing I was doing. Suddenly my husband turned to me and said, "Thelma, Mr. Walker is right. I've done everything to you that I guess I could have, but you've always stayed a good wife. If you forgive me for what I've done and how I've hurt you, I promise I will never deliberately do anything to hurt you again. It's over with her [the 'other' woman]. I'm done with this. There's nothing out there that I want more than you, and I'm not leaving my wife for anybody. I love you."

"I love you too," I told him. "But I hope you're being straight with me. I'll forgive you, but it'll take some time to forget. I want a whole husband, not a piece of a husband. If you can promise you will be that, I accept your apology."

Praise God, I can honestly say that from that point on my husband has kept his word. He has been a whole husband. He has supported me in all my endeavors. He is my prayer partner and my greatest fan. We've gone through trials related to our finances, children, health, and more since that time, but God made our marriage in heaven. He was faithful to keep His promise to bless our marriage in spite of us. That fateful day renewed our relationship with each other and solidified the marriage God had divinely orchestrated for us. Satan was playing his ugly hand in our marital affairs by creating battles of discord, unfaithfulness, bitterness, and anger. But God won all the skirmishes and ultimately the war. Now we don't look back at what was; we appreciate what is and look forward to wonderful tomorrows.

Our marriage was saved by the prayers of a few Christian friends, my praying and fasting, my husband's desire to do right, and wise counsel from Granny. I knew deep down that God had joined George and me together for life, even though I contemplated ending the marriage that one time. Praise God that I didn't! Now, every day, George and I happily celebrate more than 48 years of oneness.

All marriages may not turn out so well. Marriages do break, and some are not repaired. But God is always faithful to heal and restore broken lives. You can be sure that His love is greater than all your problems. Praise His holy name!

Prayer

Father, thank You for bringing the institution of marriage into this world. The love that a husband and a wife can enjoy reflects (if only dimly) the love Your Son has for His bride, the church. When You create a marriage in heaven, it's difficult for anything to kill it except the selfish intent of the partners spurred on by the devil. Help me remember that You have control over my marriage, and Your mighty power can solve whatever problems come along. Thank You for being a God of love and restoration. Amen.

God's Word to You

At the beginning of creation God "made them male and female. For this reason a man will leave his father and mother and be united to his wife, and the two will become one flesh." So they are no longer two, but one. Therefore what God has joined together, let man not separate (Mark 10:6-9).

Affirmation

Because of God's grace, power, and blessing, my marriage can survive Satan's attacks.

42

The Joys of Grandparenting

Have you seen the bumper sticker that reads, "If I'd known having grandchildren was this good, I would have had them first"? My husband and I can relate to that. We often get to be weekend "stabilizers" for our kids by taking care of their kids. On many a Sunday afternoon, the kids descend on us with all their luggage, baby equipment, and children. We love it!

If you're a grandparent, there is no greater legacy to leave your family for generations to come than your righteous love and faith. The apostle Paul encouraged Timothy by mentioning his bloodline of faith: "I have been reminded of your sincere faith, which first lived in your grandmother Lois and in your mother Eunice and, I am persuaded, now lives in you also" (2 Timothy 1:5).

Sweetness and tender compassion are wrapped up in my grandparenting. Even when I have to caution or reprimand one of my grandkids, I do it with an irrepressible gladness and a smile in my voice. I also make sure they know I love them enough to discipline them. I believe grandparents can play a powerful role by...

- supporting the godly teachings of their children
- setting a good example of what God expects from His disciples
- showing no favoritism toward any of the kids or grandkids
- encouraging their children, as well as the grandchildren, to seek the will of God in their decisions and choices

- training the grandchildren to fear the Lord and turn away from evil

- teaching the grandchildren to obey their parents, grandparents, teachers, and other authority figures

- helping to protect the grandchildren from ungodly influences by being aware of Satan's attempts to destroy or sidetrack them

- encouraging the children and grandchildren to attend a church where God's Word is proclaimed

- teaching the grandchildren that God loves them and has a specific purpose for their lives

- instructing the grandchildren in God's Word through conversation, family prayer, Scripture, Christian music, and family devotions

- lifting up the children and grandchildren before the Lord in constant and earnest intercession

- not interfering when the children are correcting their children

- not giving the grandchildren everything they think they want

- allowing the grandchildren to earn (by working) some of the luxuries they desire

- exposing the grandchildren to some of the finer things in life, such as theater, opera, travel, and fine dining

The great thing about being a grandparent is that you don't have to do all of these things every day. You usually get to choose when to see your children and grandchildren. My husband and I get to pamper our grandchildren, let them get away with "no harm done" antics, love them, and then leave them with their parents!

I'm thankful to God that George and I have lived long enough to see our children's children. If you have grandchildren, love them, train them, and enjoy them! And if you have grandparents still living, honor them and include them in your life. God's heart is delighted by the loving interactions of the generations.

Prayer

Dear God, You did such a marvelous thing when You established the family. The components of a father and mother, children, and grandchildren are so orderly and well designed for the good of the family unit. Thank You for the unique role You've given to Christian grandparents. Let Your light shine in me so that my grandchildren will see You and choose to trust and glorify You. Thank You for promising to bless my descendants in this generation and for generations to come. Amen.

God's Word to You

He decreed statutes for Jacob and established the law in Israel, which he commanded our forefathers to teach their children, so the next generation would know them, even the children yet to be born, and they in turn would tell their children. Then they would put their trust in God and would not forget his deeds but would keep his commands (Psalm 78:5-7).

Affirmation

God will bless my descendants when I am faithful to teach them His ways.

43

A Cheerful Giver

The apostle Paul told the Ephesian elders, "In everything I did, I showed you that by this kind of hard work we must help the weak, remembering the words the Lord Jesus himself said: 'It is more blessed to give than to receive'" (Acts 20:35). That's good theology. But how many of us find it extremely difficult to give when we're barely making ends meet? Or when we're living on a fixed income and trying to save a little for a rainy day? Perhaps we have a lot of money but are reluctant to help some people who seem to need help every time we turn around. We might wonder, *If I can make it, why can't they?*

Have you ever wondered why you are constantly in need? Do you seem to be struggling all the time? And as soon as you get a little ahead and think your financial situation is smoothing out, does something almost always come along to mess it up? The car breaks down. The plumbing leaks. The air-conditioning fails. You need to buy new equipment for your business. Something costs more than predicted. The bills are due, and you don't have enough money to cover them. Well, the Bible has answers to all of these dilemmas. I've found that God's Word concerning giving is true. God promises to reward us with blessing and protection when we give without reservation.

In Malachi 3, God accused His people of "robbing" Him by withholding their full tithes and offerings. He invited them to "test" His faithfulness by giving generously, trusting that He would "throw open the floodgates of heaven and pour out so much blessing that you will not have room enough for it" (verses 8-10). In the next verse, He also promised to "prevent pests from devouring your crops." For us, I believe those words mean that when we give to God freely, He will block or mitigate anything that threatens to consume our financial security. As we give to Him, we will have peace of mind and the ability to meet our financial obligations.

There have been a number of people whose commitment to tithing and giving to my church has been strong. The Gregorys were prime examples. Even though they had seven children to take care of, the annual report of contributions showed that they tithed out of every penny they earned. Mr. Gregory worked two or three jobs to take care of his family, yet he made sure he had time to spend with his wife and children, supporting all their activities. When the children got old enough, he took them to work at his night job so they could spend time together. That family owned their home and rental properties, always had nice clothes, and were involved in church and community activities. Every one of those seven children became a college graduate. Mrs. Gregory was a kindergarten teacher, but she didn't work outside the home until her two youngest children were old enough to go to work with her. People wondered how the Gregorys could make ends meet. I truly believe that because of their obedience to God concerning finances, God honored them with financial abundance. The Gregorys were great models of what following God's plan for giving was all about.

Another great role model was Mr. Beckett. He was a professor and an administrator in the Dallas Independent School District for many years. His education and high position in the field of education, the church, and the community didn't cloud his perspective of God's plan in the area of giving. He and his wife, Helen, traveled to far-off places often. Their two children were well educated, and now their son is a dentist and their daughter is a businesswoman. Mr. Beckett wears tailored clothes and has always driven one of the finest cars on the market. He never seems to have financial problems. Mr. Beckett is a perpetual tither and gives generously to many people. I sincerely believe he can do these things because he handles his money God's way.

Mind you, I realize that people who are not tithers can progress financially. But I have experienced the supernatural power of God with respect to my finances when I have obeyed His principles. Years ago I deliberately entered into an intense study on tithing to prove to myself that the New

Testament didn't "require" it. I wanted to find a reason not to tithe. What I found instead is that Scripture spells out three specific kinds of giving that God's people are to heed:

- The tithe that belongs to the Lord. Malachi 3:10 commands, "Bring the whole tithe into the storehouse, that there may be food in my house." We are to give part of what we have in this life directly back to God. We dare not rob Him of what is His.

- The offering that is a freewill decision. Second Corinthians 9:6-7 explains, "Whoever sows sparingly will also reap sparingly, and whoever sows generously will also reap generously. Each man should give what he has decided in his heart to give, not reluctantly or under compulsion, for God loves a cheerful giver."

- The alms for the needy. These are items such as clothing, shoes, furniture, food, that we give out of love to help less fortunate people. Deuteronomy 15:11 (NASB) commands, "For the poor will never cease to be in the land; therefore I command you, saying, 'You shall freely open your hand to your brother, to your needy and poor in your land.'"

We're no longer under the law of the Old Testament, so the 10 percent tithe isn't required. But Jesus did say we are to give. He commended the widow who gave to God sacrificially (Mark 12:42-44).

I discovered there was no scriptural way out of giving God's way! So I started giving, and I did it cheerfully. I trusted Him, proved Him, and tried Him—and He has never disappointed me. Yes, sometimes I was plagued by fear of not having enough. At other times greed reared its ugly head. I wanted to keep the money I had and get more. I'll never forget one experience. I'd started making quite a bit of money, which increased my tithe substantially. While I was soaking in the bathtub one Sunday morning debating whether or not to give "all that money to the church," I thought, *How can I expect God to give me big things when I'm not a good steward of the little things?* I regrouped right then and erased my greedy thoughts from my mind and choose to give wholeheartedly.

I remember another experience vividly. Several years ago I was asleep in a hotel in a town where I was to speak the following morning. About five o'clock in the morning I was awakened with an urge to get up and send a certain minister an offering. I had prayed several days earlier and asked God which person He wanted me to give an offering to, but was this His answer? I wrestled not only with the time of day I got the revelation but also with the amount. *Say what?* I thought. *Give that much? It's too early, God. Lemme go back to sleep, and I'll see if I still have this urge when I wake up.* But I couldn't sleep. God was trying to answer my prayer, and I was being difficult.

When I realized what was happening, I thanked God for His answer. The urge to give grew, but the joy was even greater. I wrote the check and asked the Lord to reveal the address where I was to send it. Then I turned on the television. Lo and behold, the preacher I felt led to send the offering to was on TV and his ministry's address was on the screen below his name. *Whoa!* Was that God's confirmation or what?

Back home something else happened that really confirmed God's leading. George said, "Thelma, I wrote this name and address down. We need to send this man some money." It was the same man I'd already written and mailed a check to! I told my husband about my early morning urge, and he smiled in agreement and gave me a satisfied nod. George and I had gotten the same revelation. We gave liberally and cheerfully in complete obedience to God. What joy!

A few days later, we received the news that we had a large check coming in the mail to reimburse us for money owed to us that we'd forgotten all about. Some time after receipt of that money this scripture came to me: "He who sows sparingly will also reap sparingly, and he who sows bountifully will also reap bountifully" (2 Corinthians 9:6 NASB). God was true to His Word!

Are you holding back from giving cheerfully because of fear or greed? Try God's principles. See if He keeps His word. Experience has taught me that God is the provider of everything. Both jobs and financial resources are provisions. And God promises to "supply all [our] needs according to His riches in glory in Christ Jesus" (Philippians 4:19 NASB). With that kind of assurance you and I can be generous givers. Praise the Lord!

Prayer

Father, sometimes I get lax with my giving and following Your principles regarding my finances. I allow people, places, things, fear, greed, disobedience, and stubbornness to get in the way of giving cheerfully and wholeheartedly. Sometimes I rationalize that what I know I need to give is too much or I make the excuse that the money isn't going to be used the way I think it should be. But when I remember the amounts of money I pay Uncle Sam, the times I buy things I don't really need, the things I buy for other people just because I want to, I admit that maybe my love for them is greater than my love for You. Forgive me, God. You've proven to me over and over that You will take care of all my needs. In return, I will honor You with my giving. Amen.

God's Word to You

Let the LORD be magnified, who has pleasure in the prosperity of His servant (Psalm 35:27 NKJV).

Affirmation

*I give cheerfully from the heart because I
serve a God who supplies all my needs.*

44

Family Get-togethers

Family is so important. It's great to have family and want to be around loved ones. Almost every week George and I experience blessings when our children come with their families and friends. We look for any reason to get together: Mother's Day, Father's Day (when the Wells' family reunion takes place), Easter, Christmas, Super Bowl Sunday, and every Sunday I'm in Dallas. Graduations, baby christenings, birthdays, anniversaries, baby showers, bon voyages, and even funerals are times to celebrate with a gathering at our house. There's nothing necessarily unique or spectacular about our family get-togethers, but everything we do is done in love.

Your family may not consist of a spouse, children, grandchildren, or any immediate relatives. Maybe you have extended family members or you consider your friends to be your family. Whoever your family is, they play a significant role in your well-being because you want to be bonded to somebody. *Everybody needs somebody.* That's why I believe family is so significant in God's overall plan for our lives. The family was the central unit of Hebrew society, and the concept of the family was often extended to refer to tribes, to the kingdoms of Israel and Judah, and to the Israelites as a whole.

Those of us who have accepted Jesus Christ as our Savior are part of the greatest family ever created. We belong to the family (the household) of God. God is our Father; we are His children. He accepts us, protects us, directs us, comforts us, disciplines us, loves us, and cares for us better than any human being could ever hope to do. Greater than our relationship with our personal families is our heavenly Father's relationship with us.

George and I have so much to talk about after our loved ones leave. We rehash what the babies did or said, what's happening to the "old" children. How nice their friends are. And how much everyone ate. We rejoice at the fun we had and the rushing feeling of excitement that's hard to explain unless you experience it too. But that rush is nothing compared to the holy excitement we get to enjoy as members of the household of God. Do you look forward to the day when God's entire family will get together with Him for eternity? Can you imagine the singing, shouting, and running that will take place? My sister gave me a delightful plaque that I love:

> A happy family is but an earlier heaven. Remember that children bring us up instead of the other way around. Faith is love taking the form of aspiration. Celebrate the rituals, birthdays, and anniversaries in your life with vigor and enthusiasm. Only our individual faith in freedom can keep us free. Rejoice in your loved one's triumph. Say something uplifting to one who is hanging their head. Walk hand in hand with truth and your family will follow.
>
> ANONYMOUS

Jesus Christ said, "I am the way and the truth and the life. No one comes to the Father except through me" (John 14:6). If you've accepted Jesus as your Lord and Savior and God as your heavenly Father, then we walk hand in hand in truth as members of God's family. We are kin to God!

This emphasis on being part of God's family may seem inconsequential to you. But consider how many families are decreasing because of separation of one kind or another. And for people who have no family, this connection is vital.

On the Mother's Day after the death of my mother, I had a brief glimpse of what it must feel like to be without an earthly family. For a moment I choked up when I remembered I have no living mother, grandmother, father, or grandfather. All I have left of my family members are my husband, children, grandchildren, a sister, a niece, a nephew, an uncle, and four distant cousins. As I realized that for the first time, the loneliness came. Thankfully it lasted only a moment. But in that instant, I suddenly felt the pain of the void that must be experienced by people who are apart from their loved ones.

If you haven't kept in touch with your family or if you are estranged from them, make every effort to contact them—and keep in contact with them. They are probably just as lonely for you as you are for them. Please make the phone call or go and visit. Write a letter, send a card, e-mail…and include photos. If you've been separated by a conflict, you may be the one God has assigned to bring the family back together. The tugging in your heart to revive family relationships isn't to be ignored.

God never ignores His family members. In the household of God, we never have to worry about separation or abandonment. Our Father is always available for whatever we need.

Prayer

Father, thank You for my family and so much happiness. The greatest family established is Your household of faith—the place where all Your children come and are at rest. In Your house there are no favorites, no taking sides, no fear of abandonment. In Your house we have comfort, peace, and loving care. When we finally arrive in Your presence, we'll experience a continual celebration of worship and praise with You forever and ever. Amen.

God's Word to You

You are no longer strangers and aliens, but you are fellow citizens with the saints, and are of God's household (Ephesians 2:19 NASB).

Affirmation

As a child of God, I am a valued part of His family,
and I have constant access to my Father
through the Lord Jesus Christ.

Mama T's Girls

When Lesa was in elementary school, she gave me one of the sweetest, most humbling compliments a mother can ever receive. She said, "Mama, you're a Proverbs 31 mother."

"A Proverbs 31 mother? What's that?" I asked.

"You know! A mother who tells us good things and does the good things the Bible talks about in Proverbs 31," Lesa replied.

I was surprised and pleased. And then I studied Proverbs 31 to see exactly what Lesa was talking about. When I read through it, it meant a lot to me because of the compliment. But it wasn't until years later that I absorbed the full meaning and took inventory of myself to see if I was deserving of such a comment.

Are you aware that Proverbs 31 lists 23 attributes of a godly wife and mother? This came to my attention when I was planning my first television program. Looking at a godly woman through the eyes of Lemuel's mother opened my eyes to the traits she extolled:

- perceptive

- entrepreneurial

- industrious

- competent

- cool, calm, and collected

- clever

- resourceful

- charitable

- a clear thinker

- a powerful negotiator

- a good people manager

- a warm and compassionate wife

- a financial planner

- a real estate agent

- a manufacturer

- an effective communicator

- fashion conscious

- supportive of her husband

- appropriately submissive

- proud of her family and accomplishments

- devoted to God

- good with her hands and her mind

- wise

When I examined all those attributes, I marveled at how God made women so complete that we are able, by His grace, to live up to these standards. Of course, sometimes we slip. We make mistakes. But even when we fall short of the ideal depicted in Proverbs 31, we learn how to correct our mistakes and move forward.

After asking God to help me demonstrate those godly attributes for several years, I got a chance to teach them to prospective wives and mothers. No, not with married women expecting children, but with teenagers who, in five or six years, would probably marry. Some girls at my church were sitting in the sanctuary one Saturday, apparently discussing some questions about how to conduct themselves when they thought older people were being discourteous to them. As I walked by them, they stopped me and asked to talk with me.

One of them said, "We want to find out how we can get those old people out of our business."

Now that statement got my attention! When I was a teenager nobody thought I had "business." And with these girls, I'd grown up with some of their parents. My reply to the girls was, "Yes, we sure do need to talk." I promised them I would talk to their youth group leaders or parents and schedule an appropriate time to meet. I followed through, and we settled on the next youth meeting at church as a good time to discuss their concerns.

As the time approached, I prayed for wisdom in handling the young ladies. I opened the meeting without knowing exactly how I was going to conduct it, but I did know that God knew the importance of wise counsel. With a prayer on my lips, an open mind, listening ears, and my Bible in my hand, I tackled their questions.

Apparently some of the older women in the church had rebuked the teenage girls about the too-short hemlines of their dresses, the clothes they wore to church, their makeup, and the way they wore their hair. The girls' point was that if their parents didn't mind how they looked, why was anyone else concerned? They wanted to know what they could say to people when they talked critically about how the teens looked. So that was their "business." I was so relieved! I could easily talk about this. I chatted about the biblical principle of respecting one's elders. My advice was for them to respond to the people who criticized them with a "Thank you for caring about me!" That's all they needed to say. A comment like that would show respect for the person while being noncommittal about the comments made and help the girls stay pleasant.

Talking to these girls is a piece of cake, I thought. But then the conversation continued into more sensitive and weighty issues. Things were getting so deep that we didn't have time to discuss some of their concerns in detail. I asked the girls when a good time to finish talking would be. "Tonight at your house," they said. *Tonight? My house?* I was shocked! *Oh, man! I'm not prepared for this!* But after careful consideration of their needs, I consented.

They arrived at my house at 6:30. Oh, how they needed to talk! The subjects covered ran the gamut of sex, drugs, abuse, religion, vices, school, and teen pregnancy. You name it, we talked about it. The girls had brought their Bibles. One of the requirements for coming to my house was that they had to be willing to get their answers from God's Word and not just depend on my opinion. They needed truth—God's truth!

When midnight rolled around, I finally had to ask them to call their parents to pick them up. The girls asked what they could call me. They didn't like calling me Mrs. Wells—that seemed too formal. They had heard some of the older college students call me Mama T and wondered if they could too. I said, "Sure!" So I became "Mama T" for at least a dozen young ladies. What a humbling position! These girls had enough respect for me to confide in me and ask for my advice. Their parents trusted me enough to let me be alone with their daughters and give them wise counsel.

"My" girls still weren't finished with their questions and comments. We set another date for them to come back. "Next time," they said, "we want to sleep over." I consented on one condition: Within the next 31 days they would read the book of Proverbs in its entirety. That was one chapter per day. At the end of that time, they could come back to sleep over, and we would discuss what they'd learned from their reading. If the next generation of young ladies was going to learn how to be good wives and mothers, I figured the best source of information was the Bible.

Nobody taught me how to be a wife and mother. I'd never heard of premarital counseling when I got married. Nobody had ever told me about Proverbs 31 or how to live up to those biblical expectations and still keep my sanity. Perhaps if I'd known what being a wife and mother was all about, I would have been more prepared and the shock of my responsibilities wouldn't have been so overwhelming.

Several weeks after I got married and started doing some of the things listed in Proverbs 31, I also started resenting the fact that I had to do them. I thought it was a great imposition, and I finally expressed my disillusionment to Granny. She sat me down and told me everything I was expected to do. I didn't realize at the time that she was giving me a biblical description of a virtuous woman. It sounded as if I had been handed a life sentence to work hard, make my man happy at any cost, drive a hard bargain when I wanted to buy something, wash, iron, cook, sew, clean, pick up after somebody, ad infinitum. And all that did not suit my fancy! But as I matured and learned more about what God expected of me, I realized that Proverbs 31 is not suggesting that a woman do all these things without the help and support of others. The chapter clearly describes how a good husband respects his wife and how her children call her blessed.

Older women need to be setting a positive example for girls so when young women become wives and mothers, they won't be as disillusioned and disappointed as some of us were. One of the characteristics of the woman in Proverbs 31 is her wisdom: "She speaks with wisdom, and faithful instruction is on her tongue" (Proverbs 31:26).

After my teenage friends had completed their assignment of reading Proverbs 31, they asked me when I was going to keep my end of the bargain. We scheduled a date for our sleepover. At the slumber party we had so much fun talking about their favorite passages. They were ready to have an intelligent discussion about some issues they'd been confused about before because they had started reading their Bibles with purpose. That night I made them go to bed at midnight because we had to get up and go to Sunday school the following morning. It's really interesting having a group of teenage girls in your house when your own children have moved! At least we had three bathrooms so they could use several dozen electric appliances without blowing the circuits.

That visit wasn't the last either. They wanted to come back again. Their assignment this time was to read all of Matthew 6.

My relationships with these girls continued in the most delightful way. I featured them on my television program because I believed the understanding they had gained of Proverbs 31 could help other young people and people in general. I was right. We got more requests for "the program with the girls" than for any other program I've done.

You and I never know who's watching us. We may not be aware of the example we set. It doesn't matter whether we're married or single, have children or not. What's important is exhibiting godly attributes in our lives. Even though Proverbs 31 talks about wives, it makes clear that any woman who fears the Lord will want to follow the wisdom in that passage. May we all strive to be women of noble character!

Prayer

Master, You have given me the initiative, innovation, tenacity, energy, knowledge, and everything else it takes to live a life that demonstrates the joy of following You. Help me reach out to people in Your name and share who You are. Amen.

God's Word to You

Charm is deceptive, and beauty is fleeting; but a woman who fears the LORD is to be praised. Give her the reward she has earned, and let her works bring her praise at the city gate (Proverbs 31:30-31).

Affirmation

Through desire, commitment, and prayer, I can become a virtuous woman who loves and serves others in God's name.

46

The Closet

My mother was born with a paralyzed right arm and right foot. She was also dark-skinned. My mother's mother, "Mother Dot," was from black and white ancestry. She could have passed for white if she hadn't had lanky hair. A lot of African-Americans in my grandmother's day thought "light is better" because of attitudes left over from slavery times. Dark-skinned blacks worked in the fields and were given harder jobs, while light-skinned blacks worked inside homes and secured better jobs.

Some of my relatives told me that Mother Dot was not only ashamed of her daughter's skin color, but she had also attempted to straighten out my mother's crooked limbs by pulling, massaging, and twisting. When she was unsuccessful, she punished my mother by shutting her in a closet. My mother could never do anything to please her.

When I was born, my mother was forced out of the house. My great-grandmother took me to raise when I was two years old. As I got older, "Granny" let me visit my other grandparents. Whenever my precious grandfather "Daddy Lawrence" was around, Mother Dot was fairly nice to me. But as soon as my grandfather left for work, the same closet my mother had been locked in became my place for the entire day. No water, no food.

And the closet stank. Smell it with me: It reeked of tar and sweat from the old railroad boots my grandfather wore (he was a brakeman on a railroad train in Dallas). The wool clothes in the closet trapped body odor, and the mildew in the corners as well as the heavy-duty mothballs in the clothes made me sick to my stomach. That was one stinky place!

But God is good. I'd been around church all my life and had learned many hymns by the time I was four. Just as children today learn television commercial jingles because they hear them so often, I learned the songs that had surrounded me at church. Inside the smelly closet, I sang "What a Friend We Have in Jesus" and "Jesus Loves Me." Those songs and more sustained me during the long, dark hours. As I sang, God gave me peace, and I wasn't afraid. I even sang myself to sleep sometimes.

Today I feel no sense of trauma over Mother Dot's treatment. I have no malice against her. God was with me during the abuse. And at the time I didn't even know my grandmother was being abusive. That's just the way she was. I thank God for keeping His word. He says He will strengthen us and comfort us when we are persecuted. And let's face it, there are things that happen to us in this world that we don't deserve, don't want, and can't stop. But God is faithful! As a little girl, I memorized Psalm 27. What a comfort these words were during my dark closet hours.

> The LORD is my light and my salvation—
>   whom shall I fear?
> The LORD is the stronghold of my life—
>   of whom shall I be afraid?
> When evil men advance against me
>   to devour my flesh,
> when my enemies and my foes attack me,
>   they will stumble and fall.
> Though an army besiege me,
>   my heart will not fear;
> though war break out against me,
>   even then will I be confident.
>
> One thing I ask of the LORD,
>   this is what I seek:
> that I may dwell in the house of the LORD
>   all the days of my life,
> to gaze upon the beauty of the LORD
>   and to seek him in his temple.
> For in the day of trouble
>   he will keep me safe in his dwelling;

he will hide me in the shelter of his tabernacle
    and set me high upon a rock.
Then my head will be exalted
    above the enemies who surround me;
at his tabernacle will I sacrifice with shouts of joy;
    I will sing and make music to the LORD.

Hear my voice when I call, O LORD;
    be merciful to me and answer me.
My heart says of you, "Seek his face!"
    Your face, LORD, I will seek.
Do not hide your face from me,
    do not turn your servant away in anger;
    you have been my helper.
Do not reject me or forsake me,
    O God my Savior.
Though my father and mother forsake me,
    the LORD will receive me.
Teach me your way, O LORD;
    lead me in a straight path
    because of my oppressors.
Do not turn me over to the desire of my foes,
    for false witnesses rise up against me,
    breathing out violence.

I am still confident of this:
    I will see the goodness of the LORD
    in the land of the living.
Wait for the LORD;
    be strong and take heart
    and wait for the LORD.

Whatever you've gone through or are going through, God wants you to know that He is with you and cares about your suffering. He wants you to call on Him and ask for wisdom on how to get out of abusive situations. Waiting on the Lord doesn't mean doing nothing except wait for rescue. It means doing what you know is necessary to get out of the situation while confidently anticipating God's help as you act.

The Lord cares about you! When you're in the "stinky closets" of life, trust Him to put a song in your heart.

Prayer

Father, I am so grateful I can depend on You to be with me during times when I'm mistreated and can't see a way out. Thank You for giving me the inspiration and direction to make it through the pain and humiliation of abuse. Jesus, because You were a Man of Sorrows and acquainted with grief, You understand how it feels to be persecuted by the people who should love You. Help me endure life's injustices with grace and to escape from abusive situations as soon as possible and with dignity. Amen.

God's Word to You

In the day of trouble he will keep me safe in his dwelling; he will hide me in the shelter of his tabernacle and set me high upon a rock (Psalm 27:5).

Affirmation

My loving God will comfort and strengthen me when I am hurt by this world.

47

A Ram in the Bush

Hattie and I were supposed to room together at the 1997 National Speakers Association convention in Anaheim, California. I waited for hours for her to arrive at the hotel. No Hattie. The entire night passed before I heard a word from her. About 6:15 the following morning, she called to explain that there had been a death in her family so she wouldn't be coming. She sounded composed, so there was no need for alarm.

A little after five that afternoon, I received a call from a driver in the lobby of the hotel. He said he was here to transport Hattie to a book signing in Long Beach. I didn't know anything about it, so I said, "She's not here. She had an emergency in her family and didn't come. I don't know what to tell you." Panicked, the driver asked me to call his boss, the bookstore owner, and give her the news. I did. She panicked too. She told me the book signing had been announced over the radio and in the newspaper. People were already coming into the store for Hattie's talk.

The bookstore owner asked, "Are you a speaker, Thelma? Do you have books? Can you come and stand in for Hattie?" She didn't accept any of my objections—such as nothing to wear for the occasion, too much already on my plate, and I hadn't read Hattie's book (an important point). None of these satisfied her, so I finally consented.

I went downstairs and climbed into the driver's open-air Jeep, and we sped bumpily along a Los Angeles freeway toward the customers waiting in Long Beach. With anxious anticipation, the owner stood in the downstairs doorway holding her hands together, fearful that I might not be the representative she needed for the occasion, but knowing I was the best she could get on such short notice.

As soon as I arrived and introduced myself, I asked to see the book Hattie was going to speak on. Hurriedly I read through the table of contents, glanced through a few pages, and then assured the bookstore owner I was ready.

There were about 30 people patiently awaiting Hattie's entrance. A teenager read an appropriate poem for the subject of the evening's discussion and then introduced me as Hattie's substitute. Off I went with a presentation of Hattie's book titled *Women Who Carry Their Men.* I was glad Hattie and I were such intimate friends because I was able to interject some experiences we had shared and help the audience feel they were getting a taste of the "real" Hattie.

God doesn't make mistakes. My time was divinely ordained. Hattie couldn't be there, but He sent me in her place. My testimony and advice were valued because I spoke from my experience of marital victory through many ups and downs and battle scars. I could be a godly role model for the occasion, someone the women could look to with hope.

Granny used to say when things got hectic and she didn't know what to do, "God's got a ram in the bush." She meant that we don't have to worry or be stressed when we don't see a way to meet our needs because God sees and has provided a solution. When God asked Abraham to sacrifice his son Isaac, Abraham willingly gathered the needed supplies and took Isaac up the mountain for the sacrifice. But God only wanted Abraham's *willingness.* Instead of having Abraham sacrifice his son, God provided a ram that was caught in a bush (Genesis 22). I was Hattie's ram in the bush. My willingness to substitute for her was symbolic of the price I was willing to pay to help a friend and a bookstore owner who was in need.

Jesus is our ram in the bush. He willingly endured pain and punishment so that we could be delivered from our sicknesses and sin. There has never been a more perfect substitution! Isaiah 53:4-5 NASB describes the scene:

> Surely our griefs He Himself bore,
> And our sorrows He carried;
> Yet we ourselves esteemed Him stricken,
> Smitten of God, and afflicted.

But He was pierced through for our transgressions,
He was crushed for our iniquities;
The chastening for our well-being fell upon Him,
And by His scourging we are healed.

Jesus always shows up for His appointments. He doesn't need a substitute because *He* is our substitute. He doesn't need someone to beg Him to act on our behalf. That's why He came to earth. As our High Priest, He is now seated at the right hand of God, making intercession for us, still standing in for us. Knowing that should take away all our worries and anxieties. Why should we worry? We have Jesus!

Prayer

Jesus, when I think about the tremendous price You paid for me by willingly becoming my substitute on Calvary, my heart is full of sorrow and gratitude. How can I ever thank You enough? You have set me free to live in Your strength instead of depending on mine. Although coming through for someone else can't compare to what You did when You stood in for me, Your sacrifice is an example to me. Help me imitate You by being the kind of friend to others that You are to me. Amen.

God's Word to You

He himself bore our sins in his body on the tree, so that we might die to sins and live for righteousness; by his wounds you have been healed (1 Peter 2:24).

Affirmation

When I realize the price Jesus paid to be my substitute, it's easier for me to be sacrificial for others.

48

Transforming Moments

A telephone call I received one Monday morning changed my career dramatically. Although I'd spoken to groups throughout the United States and in several foreign countries, the majority of the groups were composed of secular businesspeople. I had spoken for Christian groups all my life within my relatively small world of Dallas and a few other cities, but that's as far as my overt Christian message went. That was about to change.

The executive director of the "New Life Clinic's Women of Faith" conferences had called to ask me if she could set up an appointment to discuss the possibility of having me speak at some of the conferences. I'd never heard of Women of Faith, but I did know of the good reputation of the New Life Christian counseling clinics.

When the director came to my Dallas office, she explained that the Women of Faith conferences were the brainchild of Stephen Arterburn, the founder and chairman of the board of New Life Clinics. His idea was to bring large groups of women together to hear speakers share on living joyously in this journey called life. The current theme of the conferences was "The Joyful Journey," and women were coming by the thousands to laugh and hear and share about the grace of God.

The director told me that on the previous weekend she'd gone into a bookstore and was led to my book *Bumblebees Fly Anyway: Defying the Odds at Work and Home*. She'd become absorbed in the book and was certain God had inspired her to read it and prompted her to ask me to travel with the conference. She was frank when she told me I would be the first black woman speaker, and that little or no African-American participation had occurred up to this point. She thought I could lend a lot of credibility to the venues and, at the same time, influence women of color to become more involved.

What the director didn't know was that I'd been asking God to give me a forum where I could minister to more people at one time than I could in the corporate world. I didn't want to camouflage what I believed anymore or have to present some stale formula for success that didn't involve the Word of God. I was filled with joy at the opportunity to work in God's vineyard in a forum that was attracting women in droves. When she asked me about my availability for the months of August, September, and October, my schedule was completely open for the specific dates of the conferences. That in itself was a miracle and confirmation from God that He wanted me to be involved.

Isn't the way God works amazing? He had that June day planned for me before the foundation of the world. Before I was formed in my mother's womb, God planned my goings and comings. Praise Him!

My first "Women of Faith Joyful Journey" conference was in Allentown, Pennsylvania. I had never been part of a Christian women's conference of that magnitude. There were approximately 6000 women in attendance, and during my 45-minute speech they laughed and cried and applauded. It was a transforming time. I knew this was it! This was where God wanted me to be. This was the fulfillment of the desire He'd put in my heart. He had allowed a passion to grow in me that would be satisfied in this moment and in this venue.

When I got back to Dallas, the director called and said just what I longed to hear. "Thelma, my original thought was to have you be a regular speaker at our next year's conferences, but you were such a hit, we'd like you to join us for the rest of this year too…if your schedule will allow it. I know how busy you are. You may not have all the dates available, but will you check your schedule and let us know? If you can join us, we'll have a contract in the mail this week."

I wish you could have been a fly on the wall watching me and listening to my heart pound with excitement. I wish you could have seen the tears of joy streaming down my round cheeks, making white salt lines down my face. I wanted to jump up and do a holy dance! And God showed His perfect plan for my life again. All the dates the director wanted were open. God was transforming my life right before my eyes with an opportunity I hadn't heard of just a few short months before.

I participated in many Joyful Journey conferences and have had opportunities to be part of other conferences too. The power of God is becoming more and more evident as the speakers and attendees come together to learn more about and discuss our wonderful, omniscient, omnipotent, omnipresent God. At one Sacramento conference, 99 women accepted Christ as their personal Savior and 12,000 asked for more information! That's what these conferences are all about: winning souls for the kingdom and encouraging women to exhibit joy (a fruit of the Spirit). God's Spirit touched, healed, revived, regenerated, reestablished, and reconciled thousands of women to His way of responding to life's ups and downs through an earthly vessel like me. To quote dynamic speaker and author Bishop T.D. Jakes from an interview about the successful growth of his ministry, "It makes you look like you have a great strategy. But it's God who has a great strategy, and then you stumble onto it."[1]

Our God is a God of order. He has already determined the path each life is to take to bring glory to Him and satisfaction to our souls. Our jobs are to seek His wisdom and be open and flexible to His plans for us that may—and more than likely will—alter our lives dramatically.

Prayer

Father God, how I thank You for the significant moments in which You transform my life according to Your will. Before the foundation of the world, You ordained what I was created to do. You know exactly what will satisfy my soul. I'm so glad to know that the path I take in response to Your directions is paved and ready for travel. I never really know where You're taking me because You surprise me almost every day. But I do know You are orderly, organized, and sovereign. Therefore, I trust Your transforming moments and embrace Your will for my life. Amen.

God's Word to You

The LORD will guide you continually, and satisfy your soul in drought, and strengthen your bones; you shall be like a watered garden, and like a spring of water, whose waters do not fail (Isaiah 58:11 NKJV).

Affirmation

I trust You, God, to guide me to the activities and relationships that will satisfy my soul.

Notes

Part 1

Did You Say, My Book?
1. Thelma's book *Capture Your Audience Through Storytelling* can be found at Amazon.com.

The Doctors Had Given Up
1. The Full Life Study Bible (Deerfield, FL: Life Publishers International, 1992), 732.

Part 2

Oh, Blessed Savior
1. Frederick Whitfield, "Oh, How I Love Jesus," 1855.

The Call Up Yonder
1. The Full Life Study Bible (Deerfield, FL: Life Publishers International, 1992), 732.

Go and Make Disciples
1. Postcards, pocket cards, T-shirts, bee jewelry, and more can be purchased at my website: www.thelmawells.com.

Low Self-esteem?
1. Thelma Wells and Jan Winebrenner, *Bumblebees Fly Anyway: Defying the Odds at Work and Home* (Dubuque, IA: Kendall/Hunt Publishing Company, 1996), 76.

Transforming Moments
1. *Dallas Morning News,* religion section, Saturday, July 5, 1997.

About the Author

THELMA WELLS' life has been a courageous journey of faith. Born to an unwed and physically disabled teenager, the name on Thelma's birth certificate read simply "Baby Girl Morris." Her mother worked as a maid in the "big house" while they lived in the servants' quarters. When Thelma stayed at her grandparents' home, her mentally ill grandmother locked her in a dark, smelly, insect-infested closet all day. To ease her fear, Thelma sang every hymn and praise song she knew.

A trailblazer for black women, Thelma worked in the banking industry and was a professor at Master's International School of Divinity. Her vivacious personality and talent for storytelling attracted the attention of the Women of Faith Tour. She was soon one of their core speakers. She was named Extraordinary Woman of the Year in 2008 by the Extraordinary Women Conferences. She also received the Advanced Writers and Speakers Association's Lifetime Achievement Award in 2009.

Along with writing books, including *Don't Give In—God Wants You to Win!* Thelma is president of Woman of God Ministries. "Mama T," as she is affectionately known, helps girls and women all over the world discover Jesus and live for Him.

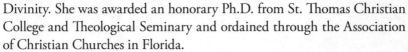

Thelma earned degrees at North Texas State University and Master's International School of Divinity. She was awarded an honorary Ph.D. from St. Thomas Christian College and Theological Seminary and ordained through the Association of Christian Churches in Florida.

Thelma and George, her husband of 48 years, enjoy spending time with their children, grandchildren, and great-grandchildren.

∞

For more information about Thelma and her ministry, check out
www.thelmawells.com.

God Calls You "Winner"!

Is stress, indecision, heartache, or fear zapping your energy? Popular speaker and author Thelma Wells says life doesn't have to be that way! Opening her heart and God's Word, she reveals how God taught her to stand tall to win against discouragement and oppression by putting on God's armor. You'll discover...

- what spiritual warfare is
- who you're fighting
- what you're accomplishing

Thelma's contagious energy and enthusiasm invites you to tackle life with a "can do" attitude. You'll find great ways to dress for successful spiritual battle by:

- fixing your hair
  (putting on the helmet of salvation in Jesus for safety)
- padding your heart
  (donning the breastplate of righteousness to confront evil)
- putting on your stomping shoes
  (stepping out in faith against the devil)

No human wins every fight, so Thelma encourages you to call on Jesus when you get tired. He wants you to win, and He actively participates with you to ensure victory.